L·THE AMAZING·E EGUME

COOKING WITH LENTILS, DRY BEANS & DRY PEAS

by Alice Jenner

THE OVERLOOK PRESS

WOODSTOCK · NEW YORK

First published in 1989 by
The Overlook Press
Lewis Hollow Road
Woodstock, New York 12498

Library of Congress or Cataloging-in-Publication Data

Jenner, Alice
  The amazing legume/by Alice Jenner
    p. cm.
  Includes index.
  1. Cookery (Peas)   2. Cookery (Beans)   3. Cookery (Lentils)
I. Title.
TX803.P4J46   1989
641.6'565—dc20   89-8634
ISBN 0-87951-364-0

INTRODUCTION

Dry beans and lentils, the food of frugality, are finally getting some respect.

Everyone knows they're cheap and filling. For years, that was the extent of a bean's status. Then, its prestige began to rise. Good restaurants added them to menus, often ranging beyond the familiar white or red beans to more exotic variegated or black beans.

The popularity of Southwestern and Mexican food and the rising interest in Cuban and Latin cooking started the bean on its way. Refried beans, pinto beans and black beans with rice became familiar. Lifestyles that focus less on meat and more on vegetable protein also played a part. Health concerns drew attention to legumes, the blanket name for dry peas, beans and lentils. People already knew legumes as an inexpensive source of cholesterol-free protein. Legumes are low in fat and sodium, and provide B vitamins and iron.

More recently, researchers have found that the soluble fiber in legumes, barley, oat and rice bran helps lower blood cholesterol levels. The good that soluble fiber does might be imagined as little brushes cleaning the arteries.

A half cup of cooked beans has approximately the cholesterol-lowering effect of one-third cup of oat bran. Research indicated that many people can lower their cholesterol by 13 to 14 percent by eating two servings of beans a day.

Nutrition aside, legumes taste good. Their mealy, rich texture and bland flavor adapt to many seasonings. From the red kidney beans in spicy chili to the white beans in a French cassoulet fragrant with thyme, beans are homey and satisfying.

Alice Jenner takes a down-to-earth approach. Her recipes are simple and inexpensive. You don't need exotic ingredients or a well-stocked kitchen. A beginner could handle most of the recipes, especially since beans take to improvisation. You can add carrots or celery or leave them out. You can vary the herbs. It still works. When Jenner calls for a meaty ham bone, I've left it out and increased the herbs or onions. It works fine. I've substituted olive oil or vegetable oil for bacon fat. Again, it works.

The lentil recipes are particularly helpful. These flat discs, about the size of a split pea, are legumes for people in a hurry. Unlike beans, they don't have to be soaked. They cook in just 30 minutes. They're delicious cooked as a pilaf with brown rice and barley.

Although legumes contain plenty of protein, they lack an amino acid that would make them a complete protein. Grains, seeds, nuts, rice or corn supply the missing amino acid. Eating legumes at the same meal with one of these foods or with a bit of meat, eggs or dairy product will provide complete protein.

Many cultures instinctively combined the complementary foods: rice with Cuban black beans, beans with tortillas, Italian pasta fagioli (beans with macaroni), French pea soup with whole grain bread, rice with tofu (beancurd) in China.

There are more than a thousand varieties of beans. The oldest domesticated beans in the Americas were found in the Ocampo caves of Mexico, dating to 4,000 B.C. Beans reached North America from Mexico. Dry beans were a staple for sailors of many countries. Because white pea beans sustained the navy, they became known as navy beans. Early Greeks and Romans not only ate beans, they voted with them. A white bean was a "yes" vote and a colored bean a "no."

In Boston, nicknamed Beantown, the traditional Saturday night supper was baked beans and brown bread. The custom began with the Puritans, who didn't cook on the Sabbath. A large pot of beans, prepared on Saturday, could be kept warm on the hearth, to provide Sunday dinner without cooking.

The earliest Bostonians cooked their beans with just a little salt pork. It probably wasn't until early in the 18th century, after the West Indies trade in molasses was established, that molasses was added to baked beans, for the flavor most of us associate with baked beans.

Beans are one of the easiest foods to grow and to store. They expand like the storybook Stone Soup. One pound (2 cups) of dry beans swells to 6 cups when cooked. One pound makes about 12 servings of soup.

Although lentils and split peas cook quickly, most bean cookery is more deliberate. You soak beans several hours or overnight, then simmer them. Beans aren't spur of the moment food. Yet there's satisfaction in such cooking, in knowing you're cooking sturdy, real food. The long simmering time is a comfortable kind of cooking. It's a soothing escape from a pressured life. It's a time to putter, maybe bake bread to go with the meal, to stir the soup pot and smell the good aromas of onions and herbs. It doesn't require much work, only that you be there. The reward is enough food, at little cost, to feed you for days.

But enough of this paean to peas and beans. On to the recipes.

—Donna S. Lee

CONTENTS

ACKNOWLEDGEMENTS

Sincere thanks to:

Atholl Forbes, Chief dietitian and the professional taste-testing panel of Regina General Hospital who gave up so many hours to taste-test and evaluate recipes. Their critical assessment and guidance was invaluable; **Lynn Minja,** Communications Consultant, Communication Branch, Saskatchewan Agriculture, for her ideas and manuscript review; **John Buchan** and **Paul Dribnenki,** Plant Industry Branch, Saskatchewan Agriculture, for their technical advice and support; **Lorrie Guillaume** for typing the manuscript; The **Saskatchewan Pulse Crop Growers' Association** for their enthusiastic support; **Alma Copeland** and **Judy Sakundiak,** home economists and wives of Pulse Crop Growers, for recipe testing; **Weight Watchers International; Alberta Agriculture; Eileen Neill,** Agricultural Canada; **Betty Lowe Janson** who has worked with lentils and dry peas for 25 years in Latah, Washington and offered many good ideas and helpful support; **Market Development Fund,** Saskatchewan Economic and Development and Trade for their generous support; **Dry Pea and Lentil Commissions,** Moscow, Idaho.

ABOUT THE AUTHOR

The Amazing Legume reflects Alice Jenner's interest in nutritional quality at modest prices without sacrificing appearance or flavor. She has devoted many years to good nutrition; studying and teaching it, working in and organizing programs to promote it.

Her studies began at the University of Manitoba, Canada where she obtained a Bachelor of Science in Home Economics. Her other nutrition qualifications include a dietetic internship from Toronto's Hospital for Children and a degree in nutrition from the University of Toronto's School of Hygiene.

Her first assignment took her to Szechwan, China where she studied the Chinese language at the University of West China, then taught home economics and dietetics to medical, dental, nursing and education students. She became the director of dietetics at the University Hospital in Szechwan and developed a diet manual for the hospital. While in China she also encouraged the establishment of a faculty of home economics at the University.

The time she spent in China gave her an opportunity to study a different culture and that culture's use of food. She saw how other cultures use meat sparingly, rely mainly on plant foods for their nutrients and energy and use spices, herbs and other seasonings to flavor their food.

She and her husband Harley returned to Canada in 1941 and she paused to raise three children, Lynda, Nancy and Hugh. During this time, like all mothers, she gained much practical experience in feeding active, growing children, balancing food likes and dislikes, staying within a budget.

She returned to a career outside the home in 1963 as nutrition consultant to Saskatchewan's Department of Public Health. Subsequently she became director of the department's nutrition division, a position she held until her retirement in 1977. From 1981 to 1983 she served as nutrition consultant to the Saskatchewan Pulse (Legume) Crop Growers' Association.

Alice Jenner's book, **Food: Fact and Folklore,** is used in Canadian schools and is one of the country's best sellers. She has written articles for the public and her peers, position papers for professional associations and publicity material for the legume crop growers.

Alice Jenner has visited countries in Asia, Africa, the Caribbean, Europe and South America plus the United States, Mexico and much of Canada. She was named to the Who's Who of Women in 1979 and is an honorary member of the Saskatchewan Dietetic Association and Saskatchewan Home Economics Association.

HISTORY AND ORIGIN OF LEGUMES

Legumes, also called pulses have been eaten for as long as historical records are available and their value as food probably predates recorded history.

Legumes were the subject of what may be the world's first nutrition survey. Over two thousand years ago their nutritional value was recognized by the author of the Biblical book of Daniel (Daniel 1, verse 12) who wrote: *"Prove thy servants I beseech Thee ten days and let him give us pulse to eat and water to drink, then let our countenances be looked upon before Thee and the countenances of the children that eat of the portion of the King's meat. At the end of ten days their countenances appeared fatter and fairer in flesh than all the children which did eat of the portion of the King's meat. Thus Melzar took away the portion of their meat, and the wine they should drink; and gave them pulses.*

The ten day nutrition survey ended in favor of the legumes or pulses. Ancient civilizations used various legume crops, such as lentils, dry peas, fababeans, and dry beans.

LENTILS

Lentils were common to the diets of the ancient Greeks, Hebrews, Egyptians and Romans. They originated from wild species that still grow in Turkey and other Middle Eastern countries.

DRY BEANS

Radiocarbon dating reveals that, about 8,000 years ago Indians in what is now the Ancash Province of Peru, cultivated the same kind of lima beans and common beans that we know today as navy beans, pinto beans, black beans and other types.

DRY PEAS

Dry peas, centuries old, have been discovered in a Neolithic village in Switzerland, in predynastic Egyptian tombs, in ruins of Troy, and buried in caves in Hungary. It is said that Aryans from the East introduced dry peas to the pre-Christian Greeks and Romans. Archaeological evidence suggests that peas were grown in the Eastern Mediterranean and Mesopotamia at least 5,000 years ago.

NUTRITIONAL VALUE

MEALS FOR MILLIONS

Lentils, peas, fababeans and dry beans are nutritious and versatile foods. The greater part of the world's people get most of their protein and other essential nutrients from vegetable sources. Millions of people live long, healthy lives by eating a mixture of legumes and cereals at the same meal, sometimes with small amounts of meat, eggs and dairy foods.

Since meat and dairy foods are expensive to produce, both in terms of money and other resources, economists and nutritionists believe that in the future, plants will supply increasing amounts of protein and energy for most people.

SPECIAL FEATURES

Legumes add variety to meals, are time saving, convenient and good tasting. Because of their bland flavor they combine well with other foods, spices, herbs and seasonings. Because they are non-sweet and notably high in fibre and iron, low in fat and sodium, pulses are useful for special diets such as low salt, low kilojoules, diabetic, high fibre, low cholesterol and high iron.

NUTRIENT CONTENT

Lentils, peas, fababeans and dry beans are excellent sources of vegetable protein, fibre, iron and energy. These legumes are good sources of Vitamin-A and the B-vitamins, riboflavin, thiamin and niacin. They have good amounts of calcium and phosphorus with some trace elements as an added bonus.

There is a scientific basis for using a combination of legume and cereal proteins. Legumes are low in methionine and high in lysine, thus complementing cereal proteins which are high in methionine and low in lysine. Thus a combination of legume and cereal proteins provide good amino acid balance in our diets.

FIBRE AND YOU

By definition fibre is not a nutrient. It supplies little or no protein, fats, vitamins, minerals or food energy. However, its presence or absence is important to your health.

Scientists have compared the eating habits of rural populations in less developed countries and found them free of certain digestive disorders common in the industrialized world. They believe that diet accounts for the difference, with fibre an important factor in protecting against a wide range of gastro-intestinal diseases, commonly seen in the Western World.

The richest sources of food fibre are whole grains, legumes, nuts, fruits and vegetables. Meats, poultry, fish, seafoods, milk and milk products, eggs, sugar and refined starches have little or none.

The reason the average diet in the Western World is low in fibre is because we eat so many highly processed foods. When flour is milled from grain, the tough outer layer of grain is eliminated. This is the fibre-rich layer. A second reason for our low-fibre diet is overuse of sugar. We should select food with starch energy and fibre for roughage and cut down on the sugar. Among the recommended foods are whole grain breads and cereals, legumes, fruits, vegetables and nuts.

Most people could easily reach the desirable goal of six to twelve grams of fibre a day by including these foods in their daily diet.

Caution: Like most things in life, moderation is a good idea. Some fibre is a must, a lot is not necessary. Take fibre from the recommended food sources every day but do not consume huge amounts of bran, nuts, and other fibre-rich foods in the interest of health. The digestive system may not be able to handle large amounts of roughage, nor do you need a surplus.

DIETARY RECOMMENDATIONS

A great deal has been written about "what to eat to be healthy". The value of good nutrition in the maintenance of health and the prevention and effective treatment of disease continues to attract increasing attention and interest.

A great fund of scientific knowledge has been built by specialists and serves as a guideline for well-balanced diets. Dietary standards and recommended nutrient intake allowances have been designed, appropriate for use by various countries around the world.

These nutrition recommendations are as follows:
1. Consume a nutritionally balanced diet
2. Avoid overweight.
3. Limit the total amount of fat, cholesterol, sugar, alcohol and salt in the diet.
4. Reduce the total amount of saturated fat in the diet and replace some of this with polyunsaturated fats.

It is as if legumes were specifically designed to meet the requirements of these recommendations. They make a positive contribution to every stated goal.

The Old Testament of the Bible records the story of Esau, who is said to have sold his birthright to his twin, but second born brother Jacob for a "potage of lentils". His was a costly transaction, but he was getting a food bargain.

COOKING LEGUMES

Things have changed for the better in the preparation of these ancient foods. In the old days legumes needed pre-soaking and a lengthy cooking of 2-3 hours. Not so today. The thinner skinned seeds need no pre-soaking and should be simmered — not boiled. Depending on age, variety and proposed use, they cook in 10-45 minutes.

How to Cook Lentils and Split Peas

1. Rinse before using.
2. Do not soak (some cookbook instructions are to the contrary).
3. Use twice the amount of liquid as lentils and split peas because lentils and split peas double in bulk with cooking.
4. Cook approximately 10-45 minutes, according to type and variety. Do not pressure cook — these legumes tend to clog the safety valve, which may cause an explosion.

How to Cook Dry Beans and Whole Peas

1. Pick over peas and beans, discard foreign matter and rinse.
2. **Always soak** beans and whole peas before cooking. **To soak** — for each cup (250 mL) beans or whole peas, add 2½-3 cups (675-750 mL) water. Let stand for 12 hours or overnight.
3. For **quick soaking**, slowly bring to a boil and boil gently for 2-3 minutes. Remove from heat and let stand 1 hour. After a quick soak, beans and peas should cook to tenderness in 1-1½ hours.
4. **To cook** — for each cup (250 mL) beans or whole peas add 2½-3 cups (625-750 mL) fresh water. When possible, use soft water. Simmer, oven bake or pressure cook according to the time given in recipe or pressure cooker instructions. They should be tender when done.
5. **Pressure Cooking** — a pressure cooker eliminates the need for overnight soaking of dried beans, and cuts cooking time to about a quarter of the traditional method. It is not, however, recommended for lentils or split peas. The cooker should be no more than 1/3 full of beans to allow for expansion — Too many beans may clog the steam vent. Cover the beans with water and add 1 Tbsp. (15ml) oil to reduce foaming. If in doubt, it is better to have too much water than too little, as dried beans absorb large amounts of water and might even cause the pressure cooker to run dry and burn the beans. The pressure cooker can be used to cook beans alone, or you may add other ingredients to make bean soup, etc. The cooking times suggested below are for 15 pounds pressure, which is appropriate for most beans.

Cooking Times For Peas, Lentils and Dry Beans

Legume	Simmer	Pressure Cook	Minimum Yield
Split peas, yellow or green	45 min.	not recommended	cooked volume from 1 cup (250 mL) = 2 cups (500 mL)
Peas, yellow or green	1½-2 hr.	3-5 min.	2½ cups (625 mL)
Lentils, green	30-45 min.	not recommended	2½ cups (625 mL)
Lentils, red	10 min.	not recommended	2½ cups (625 mL)
Lentils, salmon pink	10 min.	not recommended	2 cups (500 mL)
Lentils, slate green (French)	10-15 min.	not recommended	2 cups (500 mL)
Dry Beans	1½-2 hr.	7 min.	2½ cups (625 mL)

Green lentils were used for all the recipe testing hence the cooking time instructions. If using Red, Peach or the Slate-Green (French) lentils refer to the chart above for recommended cooking times.

After cooking, these legumes may be seasoned, buttered and eaten without further cooking, or they may be combined with other ingredients in recipes calling for cooked peas, beans or lentils.

Preparation Methods to Prevent Flatulence

Approximate cooking times are given for these legume recipes. However, cooking times vary according to the age and length of storage time. It is a good idea to keep an eye on them and adjust the cooking time appropriately.

If you find flatulence a problem, prepare the beans as follows: Boil the beans for 3 minutes and allow the beans to soak in the boiled water at room temperature for at least 4 hours. Pour off the soaking water and add fresh water. There may be a slight nutrient loss, but you may feel the flatulence risk overrides that consideration.

6. **Microwave** — place lentils in a covered microwave-safe casserole dish with twice as much water as lentils. Cook at full power until tender; cooking time depends on the amount of lentils — test after 8 minutes. For dried beans, add 8 cups of water for each pound of beans. Cook at full power 8-10 minutes, cover, and let stand 1 hour. Stir and add water, then cook at full power for 8-10 minutes. Reduce to half power and cook for another 15-20 minutes, until tender.

By discarding soaking water and using fresh water to cook the beans, you can rid the beans of two sugars (raffinose and stachyose) that cause flatulence.

METRIC CONVERSION

The basic Metric measurements are:
mL (millilitre) for measuring liquid and dry ingredients in recipes.
L (litre) for volume such as in soups and beverages.
g (gram) a unit of mass for measuring light or small food items.
Kg (kilogram) a unit of mass for measuring large or heavy foods items.
cm (centimetre) for measuring cooking utensils and thickness of food items such as meat or vegetable slices.

LIQUID AND DRY MEASURES

Imperial	Metric	Imperial	Metric
¼ teaspoon	1 millilitre	¼ cup	50 millilitres
½ teaspoon	2 millilitres	⅓ cup	75 millilitres
1 teaspoon	5 millilitres	½ cup	125 millilitres
2 teaspoons	10 millilitres	⅔ cup	150 millilitres
1 Tablespoon	15 millilitres	¾ cup	175 millilitres
1 coffee measure	25 millilitres	1 cup	250 millilitres
		4 cups	1 litre

MEASUREMENT BY WEIGHT		LIQUID MEASURE	
Imperial	Metric	Imperial	Metric
1 oz	30 grams	1 fl oz	30 mL
2 oz	55 grams	2 fl oz	60 mL
3 oz	85 grams	3 fl oz	100 mL
4 oz	115 grams	4 fl oz	125 mL
5 oz	140 grams	6 fl oz	200 mL
6 oz	170 grams	8 fl oz	250 mL
7 oz	200 grams		
8 oz	250 grams		
16 oz	500 grams		
32 oz	1000 grams		

OVEN TEMPERATURES

Fahrenheit	Celsius
250° F	120°
275° F	140°
300° F	150° Slow oven
325° F	160°
350° F	180°
375° F	190°
400° F	200° Hot oven
425° F	220°
450° F	230°

NOTE: When using ovenproof glassware, reduce oven temperature by 10°C.

METRIC OVENWARE

Utensils	Metric Volume	Closest size in centimetres	Closest size in inches or volume
Cake Pans	2 L	20 cm sq.	8 in. sq.
	2.5 L	22 cm sq.	9 in. sq.
	3 L	30.5 x 20 cm	12 x 8 in.
		22 x 33 cm rectangular	9 x 13 in. rectangular
Loaf Pans	1.5 L	20 x 10 cm	8 x 4 x 3 in.
	2 L	22 x 12 cm	9 x 5 x 3 in.
	3 L	25 x 12 cm	10 x 5 x 4 in.
Round Layer Cake Pans	1.2 L	20 x 3.5 cm	8 x 1½ in.
	1.5 L	22 x 12 cm	9 x 1½ in.
Pie Plate	1 L	22 x 3 cm	9 x 1¼ in.
Tube Pans	2 L	18 x 9 cm	7 x 3½ in.
	3 L	22 x 10 cm	9 x 4 in.
Casseroles	500 mL		20 fl oz
	1 L		1 qt
	2 L		2 qt
	3 L		3 qt

SOUPS

Hot and hearty for winter, cool and refreshing for summer, best soups are still based on home-made stocks, rich with meat trimmings and soup bones. However, there is an array of good commercial stocks and soup combinations for those who do not have the materials or time to extract soup stock. Have on hand a supply of canned, dried and frozen bases to make soup at a moments notice.

Keep a stock pot with vegetable water enriched with scraps of vegetables to dilute concentrated soups or to make a fresh soup. Learn to use herbs and seasonings to advantage. Because of their bland flavor, legumes combine particularly well with spices, herbs, blends and other foods.

Legume soups are universal favorites and for good reason: they are nutritious and delicious.

Legume Soup Notes
— Soak whole peas and beans.
— Do not soak lentils and split peas.
— Do not use a pressure cooker for lentil or split pea soups.
— A blender is a great asset.
— Salt is best added at the end of the cooking time, as salt toughens the skins of legumes.
— Legumes are best cooked in soft water.
— For easy fat removal, chill the soup and skim off the fat. Reheat.
— Legume soups may be thinned to desired consistency with stock, vegetable water, tomato juice or milk.
— Do not boil cream soups after the milk or cream has been added.

FAVORITE LENTIL SOUP

The lentils and cheese provide approximately 20 grams of protein, fibre, energy and iron and the B-vitamins, thiamin and riboflavin, vitamin A and the minerals calcium and phosphorus, with some trace elements as an added bonus.

Ingredients

1 Tbsp. (15 mL)	Vegetable oil
2 cups (500 mL)	Onions, chopped, peeled, sautéed
1 cup (250 mL)	Carrots, thinly sliced
½ tsp. (2 mL)	Thyme
½ tsp. (2 mL)	Marjoram
1-19 oz. tin (540 mL)	Tomatoes, canned chopped
1 cup (250 mL)	Lentils, washed
8 cups (2 L)	Soup stock
¼ cup (50 mL)	Sherry, dry
	Salt and pepper (to taste)
4 oz. (115 g)	Grated cheddar cheese

Sauté onion in oil. Put all ingredients except sherry and cheese into a 4-quart (4 L) Dutch oven or soup pot. Simmer for 45 minutes or until lentils and vegetables are tender. Stir in sherry. Place 1-2 Tbsp. (15-30 mL) of cheese in each bowl and top with soup.

Yield: 10 servings.

BAKED BEAN AND WIENER SOUP

This is a hearty, nourishing soup, good for camp or a cold winter day.

Ingredients

2 cups (500 mL)	Baked beans
1 cup (125 mL)	Onions, finely chopped
½ cup (125 mL)	Celery, chopped
2 cups (500 mL)	Tomatoes, canned, crushed
6 cups (1.5 mL)	Soup stock
2 Tbsp. (30 mL)	Margarine or butter
2 Tbsp. (30 mL)	Flour
	Salt and Pepper (to taste)
4	Wieners, thinly sliced

Mash beans. Combine beans, onions, celery, tomatoes and seasoning with soup stock. Simmer in soup pot for 1 hour.

Blend margarine and flour and smooth with liquid. Stir into soup and simmer for 5 minutes. Adjust consistency and seasoning. Add thinly sliced wieners to soup. Serve hot.

Yield: 8-10 servings.

19

BASIC CREAM OF LENTIL SOUP

This is a mild cream of lentil soup. If you prefer it with more flavor, add ½ tsp. (2 mL) lemon juice or a slice of lemon to each serving.

Ingredients

2 cups (500 mL)	Green lentils
1 qt (1.25 L)	Chicken stock
1 qt (1.25 L)	Water
2	Onions, medium, chopped
2	Potatoes, medium, chopped
3 Tbsp. (45 mL)	Butter or margarine
2 Tbsp. (30 mL)	Flour
2 cups (500 mL)	Milk, whole
	Salt (to taste)
	Pepper, white (to taste)
	Sour cream and grated lemon rind

Cook together in a Dutch oven or stock pot, the lentils, chicken stock, water and vegetables—about 45 minutes, then blend thoroughly until very smooth.

Make a white sauce of butter and flour. Add to the soup pot and simmer for 5 minutes. Add milk, salt and pepper to taste. Top with a little sour cream and sprinkle with grated lemon.

Yield: 12 servings.

BEEF BROTH

Ingredients

2 lb (1 kg)	Marrow bones, shin bones or other bones
1	Onion, chopped, large
6	Pepper corns
1	Carrot, thickly sliced
	Salt (to taste)
1	Bay leaf
½ tsp. (2 mL)	Oregano
8 cups (2 L)	Water

Put the bones in a large saucepan, and cover with water. Bring to the boil, skim off the scum that rises to the top. Add the other ingredients, simmer for 2-3 hours. Add more water if needed to keep bones covered. Strain the stock, cool, skim off fat.

Yield: 6 cups (1.5 L)

CHICKEN STOCK

A well-flavored home-made stock may be used in sauces, soups and casseroles. The flavor can never be matched by a cube or a spoonful of stock dry mix.

Ingredients

	A fowl or the bones of a
1	**cooked or raw chicken**
1	**Onion**
1	**Leek**
2	**Clelery stalks**
1	**Parsnip**
1	**Carrot**
½	**Lemon, grated rind only**
	Salt (to taste)
8	**Pepper corns**
8 cups (2 L)	**Water**

Put fowl or carcass and giblets in soup kettle with all the vegetables cleaned and sliced, lemon rind, salt, pepper corns and water. Simmer gently for about 2 hours. Remove from heat, strain out chicken bones and vegetables. Chill, remove fat.

Yield: 6 cups (1.5 L)

COUPALENTINI

Ingredients

1	Meaty ham bone
12 cups (3 L)	Water
1	Bayleaf, large
10 oz (284 mL)	Tomato soup
	Add a variety of diced vegetables (onions, celery, carrots, potatoes, turnip, (to taste)
1 cup (250 mL)	Green lentils
	Salt, pepper, basil, oregano (to taste)

TOPPING: Grated mozzarella cheese and crumbled bacon

Simmer all ingredients until lentils and vegetables are tender, approximately 1 hour. Serve topped with grated cheese and crumbled bacon.

Yield: 8-10 servings.

CURRIED CREAM OF LENTIL SOUP

Ingredients

3 Tbsp. (45 mL)	Butter or margarine
3 Tbsp. (45 mL)	Flour
1-2 tsp. (5-10 mL)	Curry powder
20 oz. (568 mL)	Consommé, undiluted
1/4 cup (50 mL)	Onions, chopped
1 1/2 cups (375 mL)	Lentil purée
1 1/2 qt (1.8 L)	Whole milk
	Salt (to taste)
	Pepper, white (to taste)

Blend butter or margarine, flour and curry powder. Remove pan from heat and gradually blend in 1 cup (250 mL) hot consommé, stirring vigorously to mix flour and liquid thoroughly. Pour in the rest of the consommé and bring to a simmer.

Add onions to lentil purée, purée again. Stir well, add other ingredients. Heat, but do not boil.

Adjust seasonings.

Yield: 10 servings.

EAST INDIAN LENTIL SOUP

Ingredients

2 cups (500 mL)	Lentils, dry
1	Lamb shank, meaty
2 Tbsp. (30 mL)	Vegetable oil
½ cup (125 mL)	Onion, chopped
1 cup (250 mL)	Apples, peeled
½ cup (125 mL)	Celery, chopped
2	Garlic cloves, minced
12 cups (3 L)	Chicken bouillon
½ cup (125 mL)	Catsup
1-2 tsp. (5-10 mL)	Curry powder
1 tsp. (5 mL)	Salt
¼ tsp. 1 mL)	Pepper

TOPPING: toasted coconut

Brown lamb shank in oil in heavy saucepan, remove — set aside. Sauté onions, apples, celery and garlic in pan, stir frequently until onions are clear. Combine all ingredients and simmer for 1 hour or until all ingredients are tender.

Remove lamb shank from bone, cut into small pieces and return meat to soup. Adjust consistency and seasoning. Serve hot, garnished with toasted coconut.

Yield: 11-12 servings.

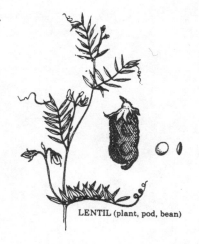

LENTIL (plant, pod, bean)

FARM AND HOME WEEK PEA SOUP

Ingredients

3 cups (750 mL)	Whole yellow peas, washed
10 cups (2.5 L)	Water, soft
½ lb (250 g)	Bacon or ham chopped
1	Hame bone
½ cup (125 mL)	Celery, diced
1 cup (250 mL)	Onion, chopepd
¼ tsp. (1 mL)	Savory
1	Bayleaf
1 tsp. (5 mL)	Salt

Boil peas in soft water for 2 minutes. Remove from the heat and let stand for at least 1 hour. Bring to boil again, add remaining ingredients except salt, reduce heat and simmer for 2 hours, stirring often.

Remove bayleaf, ham bone and add the salt. Cut the meat from the ham bone and add back to the soup.

Yield: 10 servings.

FRENCH PEA SOUP

Serve this on a cold winter day. It is a very nourishing soup, rich with the flavor of ham, bacon and spices.

Ingredients

1½ cups (375 mL)	Split peas, green or yellow
6 cups (1.5 L)	Chicken stock
1	Ham bone
¼ lb (115 g)	Bacon, crisp
2 Tbsp. (30 mL)	Butter or margarine
2 cups (500 mL)	Carrot, peeled, chopped
1	Onion, medium chopped
	Salt and Pepper (to taste)
1	Bay leaf
¼ tsp. (1 mL)	Thyme
¼ lb (115 g)	Ham, cubed

Cook the peas with the ham bone in chicken stock for 45 minutes or until tender. Cook bacon, until crisp. Remove from pan. Add butter to bacon fat and cook carrots and onion until soft.

Add vegetables and seasonings to the soup pot and simmer until vegetables are cooked. Remove ham bone and bay leaf. Purée the soup. Add ham cubes and reheat.

Serve hot.

Yield: 6 servings.

GAZPACHO SOUP

This is a summer delight — chilled vegetable soup with lentil purée to add body, protein and other essential nutrients.

Ingredients

1 cup (250 mL)	Lentil purée
3	Tomatoes, large, chopped
½ cup (125 mL)	Onions, chopped
1	Cucumber, medium, chopped
1	Green pepper, chopped
1	Green chili, small, chopped
1	Garlic clove, diced
48 oz (1.5 L)	Tomato juice
⅓ cup (75 mL)	Lime or lemon juice
2 tsp. (10 mL)	Salt
½ tsp. (2 mL)	Basil
1 tsp. (5 mL)	Dill sed
½ tsp. (2 mL)	Tarragon
¼ tsp. (1 mL)	Paprika

Blend solid ingredients throughly in the blender, mix with lentil purée and tomato juice. Add lemon juice and spices, chill well before serving.

May be served with an ice cube in each bowl. Garnish with sour cream and horseradish.

Yield: 10 servings.

LEMONY PEA SOUP

To make a typically North African soup use yellow split peas. Green split peas are equally good.

Ingredients

1 cup (250 mL)	Split peas
1 cup (250 mL)	Celery, sliced
4 cups (1 L)	Chicken stock
½ tsp. (2 mL)	Salt
¼ tsp. (1 mL)	Pepper
1 tsp. (5 mL)	Cumin, ground
2-3 Tbsp. (30-40 mL)	Lemon juice
2 Tbsp. (30 mL)	Margarine
2 Tbsp. (30 mL)	Flour

Cook the peas and celery in the chicken stock for 45 minutes or until peas are tender. Purée. Add the seasonings. Add the flour to the melted margarine, use a small amount of soup to thin, add to the soup and simmer for 5 minutes.

Serve with garlic bread.

Yield: 4 servings.

LENTIL HAM SOUP

This hearty soup was served at an agricultural field day to more than 100 hungry men. Judging by the comments it must have really 'touched the spot'.

Ingredients

1 cup (250 mL)	Lentils, washed
1	Meaty hambone
1	Bay leaf, large
8 cups (2 L)	Water, to make stock
1 cup (250 mL)	Onions, chopped, sautéed
½ cup (125 mL)	Celery, sliced
1 cup (250 mL)	Potatoes, diced
½ cup (125 mL)	Carrots, sliced
19 oz (540 mL)	Tomatoes, canned, undrained, chopped
1	Garlic clove, minced
¼ tsp. (1 mL)	black pepper
½ tsp. (2 mL)	Oregano
½ tsp. (2 mL)	Basil
	Salt (to taste)

Mozzarella cheese, grated
to top as needed

Cook a meaty ham bone in water with the bay leaf. When meat is tender cut the ham off the bone, cube it and put it to one side.

Sauté the onions and celery until tender. Add all ingredients to the broth and simmer for 45 minutes until the lentils and vegetables are tender.

Add the meat from the ham bone. Adjust the seasonings and consistency. Serve topped with mozzarella cheese.

Yield: 10 servings.

LENTIL WIENER SOUP

This hearty soup has a wonderful flavor. Great for camp.

Ingredients

1 cup (250 mL)	Lentils, washed
2 slices	Bacon, chopped
½ cup (125 mL)	Onion, diced
1 cup (250 mL)	Celery, chopped
½ cup (125 mL)	Carrot, chopped
8 cups (2 L)	Water or soup stock
2 cups (500 mL)	Tomatoes, canned
1	Bayleaf
6	Wieners
	Salt and pepper to taste

Sauté bacon and onion. Place all ingredients except wieners in a large stock pot and simmer until tender about 45 minutes. Add sliced wieners, salt and pepper and continue cooking for about 10 minutes.

Yield: 8-10 servings.

MAIN DISH MINESTRONE SOUP

Ingredients

1 cup (250 mL)	Dry navy beans
2½ cups (625 mL)	Water
8 cups (2 L)	Liquid from beans plus water
19-oz can (540 mL)	Tomato juice
½ cup (125 mL)	Onion, chopped
½ cup (125 mL)	Celery, sliced
1 cup (250 mL)	Zucchini, cubed
1 cup (250 mL)	Cabbage, coarsely chopped
1 cup (250 mL)	Turnip, diced
1	Garlic clove, crushed
1 tsp. (5 mL)	Salt
½ tsp. (2 mL)	Pepper
½ tsp. (2 mL)	Basil
2 oz. (55 g)	Spaghetti, uncooked, broken in quarters
5 tsp. (25 mL)	Cheese, Parmesan

Soak beans in water overnight. Drain, reserving liquid. Bring beans and liquid from beans plus water to a boil. Reduce heat. Cover and simmer 1 hour or until beans are tender.

Add remaining ingredients except spaghetti and cheese. Add spaghetti and cook until tender — 15 minutes. Sprinkle with cheese before serving.

Yield: 8 servings.
Courtesy of Agriculture Canada

NUTMEG CREAM OF LENTIL SOUP

An elegant looking soup when topped with cream and nutmeg. Perfect for a dinner party.

Ingredients

1 cup (250 mL)	Lentils, washed
1 qt (1.25 L)	Chicken or ham stock
1 cup (250 mL)	Onion, chopped, sautéed
½ tsp. (2 mL)	Thyme
1 Tbsp. (15 mL)	Butter
1 Tbsp. (15 mL)	Flour
2 cups (500 mL)	Milk, whole
	Salt and white pepper (to taste)
2 Tbs. (30 mL)	Lemon juice
½ cup (125 mL)	Cream
	Nutmeg, grated

Cook the lentils in the stock for 45 minutes. Sauté the onion, add thyme. Purée the lentils and onion.

Make a white sauce of butter, flour and milk. Add seasonings. Combine the purée, white sauce and lemon juice. Heat but do not boil. Serve, topped with a spoonful of cream and grated nutmeg.

Yield: 8 servings.

SAK'S LENTIL SOUP

This recipe was developed by pulse crop grower Don Sakundiak. It is substantial enough for a cold day lunch.

Ingredients

½ lb (250 g)	Beef, ground
4	Bacon strips
6 cups (1.5 L)	Soup stock
19 oz (540 mL)	Tomato juice
½ cup (125 mL)	Carrots, thinly sliced
½ cup (125 mL)	Onions, chopped
1	Garlic clove, minced
½ cup (125 mL)	Celery, sliced
½ cup (125 mL)	Cabbage, chopped
½ tsp. (2 mL)	Oregano
½ tsp. (2 mL)	Basil
¼ tsp. (1 mL)	Black pepper, ground
1 Tbsp. (15 mL)	Soy sauce
	Salt (to taste)
⅔ cup (150 mL)	Lentils, washed
1	Potato, chopped

Brown beef with chopped bacon. Sauté onion and garlic. Add all ingredients. Simmer until tender — about 45 minutes. Adjust seasonings and consistency.

Yield: 12 servings.

SLOW COOKER LENTIL SOUP

Just add thick slices of brown bread and a bowl of fresh fruit. Busy moms will have a hearty, nourishing and complete lunch ready for a "come and go" family.

Ingredients

1 cup (250 mL)	Lentils, washed
2 cups (500 mL)	Water
6 cups (1.5 L)	Chicken or beef stock
1 cup (250 mL)	Wieners, sliced
2 cups (500 mL)	Carrots, chopped
1 cup (250 mL)	Onions, chopped
1½ cups (375 mL)	Potato, diced
½ tsp. (2 mL)	Salt
¼ tsp. (1 mL)	Pepper

Cook lentils in water 25 minutes. Do not drain. Put lentils and all other ingredients in a slow cooker. Cover and cook at low for 6-8 hours.

Yield: 8 servings.

SMOKED HAM AND BLACK BEAN SOUP

The spicy-smokiness of the ham and the nutritious heartiness of the beans combine to form the basis of a meal. Add a dark, multi-grain bread, green salad and a jug of fruit juice or ale to complete it.

Ingredients

2 cups (500 mL)	Dried black beans
10 cups (2.5 L)	Water, cold
1	Onion, large, peeled, chopped
3	Celery stalks and leaves, chopped
1	Bay leaf, large
2 or 3	Ham hocks, smoked
2 Tbsp. (30 mL)	Margarine
2 Tbsp. (30 mL)	Flour
2 Tbsp. (30 mL)	Vinegar, red wine
4	Eggs, hard cooked, chopped
	Salt and freshly ground black pepper (to taste)
1	Lemon, sliced thinly

Wash beans. Place beans, water, onion, celery, bay leaf and ham hocks in a large soup pot. Bring to the boil, stirring carefully. Lower the heat and simmer for about 3 hours or until beans are tender.

Remove the ham hocks and reserve. Discard the bay leaf. Purée the soup in a blender. Add liquid as needed. Dice the meat from the ham hocks and add back to soup. Bind with margarine and flour smoothed with liquid.

Before serving stir in the vinegar add chopped eggs. Serve in individual soup bowls, garnished with a slice of lemon and a sprinkling of parsley.

Yield: 8-10 servings.

SPLIT PEA SOUP

For 10 hungry appetites you will need:

Ingredients

1½ cups (357 mL)	Split peas, yellow or green
	Meaty ham bone or pork hocks
8 cups (2 L)	Water
1	Onion, chopped
1 cup (250 mL)	Celery, chopped
2	Carrot, raw diced
1	Bay leaf, large
1	Garlic clove
⅛ tsp. (0.5 mL)	Oregano
	Salt and pepper (to taste)
2 Tbsp. (30 mL)	Butter or margarine
2 Tbsp. (30 mL)	Flour

Combine all ingredients except butter and flour in a soup pot. Bring to the boil. Remove ham bone and take off meat; cut into small pieces and add back to soup. Thin, if necessary by stirring in water, milk or cream to the heated soup, when ingredients are cooked to tenderness.

Melt butter, blend in flour and smooth with a bit of the soup mixture, stir into the soup, simmer for 5 minutes. Correct seasoning.

Yield: 10 servings.

TURKISH LENTIL SOUP

A smooth cream soup with a delicate flavor.

Ingredients

1 cup (250 mL)	Lentils, washed
¼ cup (50 mL)	Butter
1 cup (250 mL)	Carrot, thinly sliced
1 cup (250 mL)	Onion, chopped
1 cup (250 mL)	Celery, chopped
4 cups (1 L)	Chicken stock
2 Tbsp. (30 mL)	Flour
3 cups (750 mL)	Milk, whole
2	Egg yolks
1-2 tsp. (5-10 mL)	Coriander, ground
	Salt (to taste)
	Pepper, white (to taste)
1½ Tbsp. (20 mL)	Lemon juice

Melt half the butter and cook the carrot, onion and celery gently for a few minutes. Stir in the lentils and cover with the chicken stock. Simmer for 45 minutes. Blend to a smooth purée.

Blend flour and remaining butter. Smooth with a little soup stock and add to the soup pot. Simmer for 5 minutes. Stir in milk. Remove from heat and beat in the beaten egg yolks.

Add the coriander, salt, pepper and lemon juice to the puréed lentils and gradually add the white sauce. Reheat. Adjust the seasonings. Do not boil. Serve with toast, crackers or garlic bread.

Yield: 8 servings.

MAIN·DISHES

These main dishes contain protein sufficient for body needs and are lower in calories and fat than meals built primarily around animal-protein. The recipes in this section supply a good amount of protein but not an overload.

There are recipes designed to satisfy both vegetarian and meat lovers. Take your choice.

BAHAMIAN LENTILS

Ingredients

1½ cups (375 mL)	Lentils
4 cups (1 L)	Water
1¾ lb (850 g)	Pork shoulder, cubed
1	Onion, medium, chopped, sautéed
1	Garlic cloves, minced
4	Tomatoes, peeled, chopped
2 tsp. (10 mL)	Salt
¼ tsp. (1 mL)	Pepper
1 tsp. (5 mL)	Coriander seeds, crushed
3	Bananas, split
6	Pineapple slices

Simmer lentils in water until tender. Do not drain. Cover pork cubes with cold water and simmer for 1 hour. Add onion, garlic cloves and tomatoes to pork mixture. Simmer until it has a sauce-like consistency.

Add undrained lentils, salt, pepper and coriander. Simmer for a further 30 minutes. Add fruit just before serving and simmer until fruit is warm.

Yield: 10 servings.

BAKED BEANS

This North American favorite was a regular Saturday night reminder of 'home', when we served baked beans and fresh brown bread during a 7 year sojourn in western China.

Ingredients

2½ cups (625 mL)	Beans, dry, white
6 cups (1.5 L)	Cold water
1 Tbsp. (15 mL)	Oil
1 cup (250 mL)	Onion, chopped
½ lb (250 g)	Salt pork, cubed
¼ cup (50 mL)	Sugar, dark brown
¼ cup (50 mL)	Molasses
1 tsp. (5 mL)	Mustard, dry
1 tsp. (5 mL)	Salt

Cook the beans in unsalted boiling water in a large sauce pan. Add oil to reduce foaming. Bring to a full rolling boil; boil covered for 2 minutes. Set aside for 1 hour.

Return beans to a boil, reduce heat; simmer, covered for 1 hour. Drain, reserving liquid.

Use a heavy lidded bean pot and put onions on the bottom. Cover with beans and other ingredients mixed with them, including the liquid. Cover, bake for 2½ hours or until beans are tender at 300°F (150°C). Add more liquid during the baking time if needed — do not let them get dry. Bake uncovered for the final 30 minutes.

Yield: 8 cups.

BEAN POT

BEAN BURGER

A delightful version of an old favorite.

Ingredients

½ lb (250 g)	Ground Beef
½ lb (250 g)	Pork sausage
14 oz (398 mL)	Baked beans, canned
5½ oz (156 mL)	Tomato paste, canned
½ tsp. (2 mL)	Oregano
1 tsp. (5 mL)	Mustard, prepared
¾ cup (175 mL)	Cheese, grated
6	Buns, hamburger

Brown ground beef and pork together in a fry pan. Drain off excess fat. Add other ingredients, mix well, heat thoroughly. Divide mixture and spread evenly on bun halves. Top each with 1 Tbsp. (15 mL) grated cheese. Broil until cheese melts.

Yield: 12 bean burgers.

BEAN MEDLEY

Company coming? Serve this by itself with crusty brown buns and a green salad. Ham is a delicious addition to the meal.

Ingredients

1	Green pepper, diced
½	Onion, large, mild, sliced
48 oz (1.5 L)	Pork and beans, canned
14 oz (398 mL)	Kidney beans, canned, drained
14 oz (398 mL)	Lima beans, green, canned drained
1 cup (250 mL)	Mushrooms fresh or canned drained
	A little salt pork or bacon, chopped
2 Tbsp. (30 mL)	Worcestershire or soy sauce
½ cup (125 mL)	Brown sugar
¼ cup (50 mL)	Vinegar
1 tsp. (5 mL)	Mustard, dry

Sauté green pepper and onion until tender. Combine all ingredients and simmer in a covered slow oven 250°F-300°F (120°C-150°C) for 2 hours.

Yield: **10 servings without ham**
16 servings with ham

HAM AND BEAN SANDWICH SPREAD

Use your blender for this one.

Ingredients

2 cups (500 mL)	Baked beans
1 cup (250 mL)	Ham, cooked, chopped
½ cup (125 mL)	Celery, chopped
2 Tbsp. (30 mL)	Chili sauce
1 tsp. (5 mL)	Horseradish
¾ tsp. (3 mL)	Salt

Combine ingredients together lightly, adding liquid if necessary. Blend until smooth. Serve on crackers, open faced sandwiches or as a sandwich filling.

Yield: 6 servings.

MEXICANOS

Broil or grill hamburgers. Place on buns or corn bread slices. Top with baked beans or chili. Garnish with pickles or raw vegetables.

OPEN-FACED BEAN SANDWICH

Ingredients

2 Tbsp. (30 mL)	Salad oil
½ cup (125 mL)	Onion, mild, chopped
28 oz. (796 mL)	Beans, baked, canned
3 cups (750 mL)	or home baked
½ cup (125 mL)	Olives, stuffed
4 slices	Rye bread
4 slices	Cheese

Cook onion in oil until tender, stir in beans and olives. Heat. Toast bread, top with cheese slices, broil until cheese melts. Top with bean mixture.

Yield: 4 servings.

BLENDER BEAN DIP

Ingredients

¾ cup (175 mL)	Beans, cooked
½ cup (125 mL)	Lemon juice
2 Tbsp. (30 mL)	Mayonnaise
1 tsp. (5 mL)	Worcestershire or soy sauce
1 tsp. (5 mL)	Chili pepper, canned, seeded
¾ tsp. (3 mL)	Salt
3 Tbsp. (45 mL)	Green onions, chopped

Place all ingredients, except 1 Tbsp. (15 mL) green onions, in blender container. Blend until smooth, or mash beans to purée and mix with remaining ingredients. Place in serving dish and garnish with green onions. Serve as dip with fresh, raw vegetables.

Yield: 1½ cups.

CASSOULET OF BEANS

Cassoulet preparation can be a very complicated and lengthy procedure. Here is a relatively simple one with a delicious flavor combination of pork, lamb, sausage and beans.

Ingredients

2½ cups (625 mL)	Dry beans, white
8 cups (2 L)	Water
4 oz (115 g)	Salt pork
1 cup (250 mL)	Onion, chopped
¼ tsp. (1 mL)	Thyme
1	Bay leaf
1 lb (500 g)	Pork shoulder, boneless, cut into bite-size cubes
1 lb (500 g)	Lamb shoulder, boneless, cut into bite-sized cubes
	Oil
1	Garlic clove, minced
½ cup (125 mL)	Tomato sauce
1 cup (250 mL)	Chicken broth
8 oz (250 g)	Sausage, Polish or Italian sliced
	Salt and pepper (to taste)
1 cup (250 mL)	Bread crumbs, fresh
2 Tbsp. (30 mL)	Parsley, fresh, chopped

Pick over beans and wash them. Cover with water and boil 2 minutes. Remove from heat and let stand 3 hours. Do not drain — or if drained, replace the drain water with an equal amount of fresh, preferably soft water. Add salt pork, ½ cup (125 mL) chopped onions, thyme and bay leaf to beans. Cover and simmer on top of the stove or in the oven for 1 hour until beans are tender. Add water if necessary to keep the beans covered with liquid while cooking.

Brown pork and lamb in oil, separately; remove meat with a slotted spoon and put in a casserole. Brown the second ½ cup (125 mL) onions and garlic. Add to the meat. Add broth and tomato sauce, cover and bake in a 375°F (190°C) oven for 1 to 1½ hours or until meat is tender.

. . . continued . . .

Pour or spoon off excess fat from meat and combine the meat and bean mixtures. Stir in the sliced sausage. Adjust seasoning and consistency by adding a little broth or water if necessary. Pour into a baking dish such as a 9 x 13 x 2 in. (22 x 33 cm) buttered lightly. Mix fresh bread crumbs and parsley, sprinkle over bean mixture. Bake in a 375°F (190°C) oven for about 1 hour until the mixture is hot and bubbly and the crumbs nicely browned.

Yield: 8 servings.

CHEESE LENTIL RAREBIT

Easy company fare.

Ingredients

2 Tbsp. (30 mL)	Green pepper
2 Tbsp. (30 mL)	Butter or margarine
1 cup (250 mL)	Tomato juice or beer
2 cups (500 mL)	Cheddar type cheese, grated
2 cups (500 mL)	Lentils, cooked
1	Egg, well beaten
½ tsp. (2 mL)	Mustard, dry
	Salt (to taste)
	Paprika (to taste)

Cook green pepper in butter until tender. Add tomato juice or beer at room temperature and cheese; stir until cheese melts. Combine lentils and egg; add to mixture. Add mustard and salt. Heat, stirring constantly.

Serve very hot on whole wheat toast points. Sprinkle with paprika.

Yield: 6 servings.

CANADIAN BAKED LENTILS

Baked lentils are good served with brown bread and relishes, or make open-faced sandwiches from this mixture, topped with a generous sprinkling of cheese. This is a good dish for barbecues.

Ingredients

2 cups (500 mL)	Lentils, washed
2 Tbsp. (30 mL)	Onion, minced
4 cups (1 L)	Water
½ cup (125 mL)	Catsup
2 Tbsp. (30 mL)	Sugar, brown
1 tsp. (5 mL)	Worcestershire sauce
1 tsp. (5 mL)	Mustard, dry
¼ cup (50 mL)	Molasses
2 tsp. (10 L)	Salt
4 slices	Bacon

Cook lentils in water for about 30 minutes. Without draining the lentils stir in the other ingredients and top with the bacon slices. Cover and bake for 30 minutes. Uncover during the last few minutes to brown bacon.

Yield: 10 servings.

BEAN AND TOMATO CHOWDER

A great stretcher for barbecues and group gatherings.

Ingredients

28 oz can (796 mL)	Beans, baked, canned
28 oz can (796 mL)	Tomatoes, canned
2 Tbsp. (30 mL)	Barbecue sauce
¼ tsp. (1 mL)	Mustard, dry

Combine all ingredients in a heavy sauce pan. Heat thoroughly over low heat.

Yield: 7 cups.

CASSOULET OF LENTILS

This is a hearty main-course casserole. Serve it with crusty buns, a green salad and a good red wine.

Ingredients

2 cups (500 mL)	Lentils
4 cups (1 L)	Water for cooking
1 cup (250 mL)	Carrots
1 cup (250 mL)	Onion
1 cup (250 mL)	Celery
3 Tbsp. (45 mL)	Flour
½ cup (125 mL)	Wine, red or white
1½ cups (375 mL)	Meat stock or bouillon
1	Bay leaf, crushed
¼ tsp. (1 mL)	Oregano
	Salt and pepper (to taste)
2 lbs (1 kg)	Pork shoulder butt or Lamb shoulder, cubed
8 oz (250 g)	Sausage — Polish or Italian sliced
½ cup (125 mL)	Bread crumbs, fresh
	Parsley, for garnish
3 Tbsp. (45 mL)	Onions, green, chopped

Cook the lentils in water for 30 minutes or until tender. Drain. Sauté the carrots, onions and celery in oil until tender. Blend flour into the vegetable mix and add the wine, stock and seasonings. Simmer for 5 minutes. Cube the meat into bite-size pieces, spread in a roasting pan and brown in a 450°F (230°C) oven for 25-30 minutes. Turn the meat occasionally and baste with the juices in the pan. Combine the lentils and wine sauce and place in a 9 x 13 x 2 in. (22 x 33 cm) casserole. Add the meat and sausage and push the pieces into the lentil mixture. Pour meat fat from the roasting pan, add a little wine or bouillon to the pan to collect the residual meat juices and pour over the casserole. Add the bread crumbs, parsley and green onions over all. Bake in a 375°F (190°C) oven for about 1 hour or until mixture is hot and bubbly.

Yield: 6 servings.

CHICKEN-LENTIL CURRY

Ingredients

½ cup (125 mL)	Lentils, washed
2 Tbsp. (30 mL)	Oil
1 cup (250 mL)	Apple, finely chopped, peeled
⅔ cup (150 mL)	Green onion, with tops
1 cup (250 mL)	Celery-diced
1	Garlic clove, minced
2 Tbsp. (30 mL)	Cornstarch
2-3 tsp. (10-15 mL)	Curry powder
½ tsp. (2 mL)	Salt
¾ cup (175 mL)	Chicken broth
2 cups (500 mL)	Milk
2 cups (500 mL)	Chicken, cooked, diced
1 cup (250 mL)	Mushrooms, fresh or canned, sliced

Cook lentils 30 minutes — drain (See page 13). Sauté apple, celery, onion and garlic in oil. Cook until onion is tender. Combine cornstarch, curry, salt and cold broth. Cook and stir until mixture thickens and bubbles.

Stir in milk, lentils and chicken. Add mushrooms — cook a little longer. Serve on rice ring or with plain, fluffy rice.

Yield: 6 servings.

CURRIED RICE WITH LENTILS

This is good by itself, topped with yoghurt, raisins, sunflower seeds, peanuts or chutney, or it makes a splendid stuffing for tomatoes or green peppers. Make double the recipe and serve it both ways.

Ingredients

1-2 Tbsp. (15-30 mL)	Cooking oil
½ cup (125 mL)	Onion, medium
3 cloves	Garlic, minced
	Ground ginger or fresh minced
1 slice	ginger
¼ tsp (1 mL)	Turmeric
½ tsp. (2 mL)	Curry powder
1 cup (250 mL)	Rice, brown, washed
¾ cup (175 mL)	Lentils
4 cups (1 L)	Water
2	Bouillon cubes, chicken
	Salt (to taste)
½ cup (125 mL)	Raisins
¼ cup (50 mL)	Sunflower seeds
2	Apples, medium, tart

TOPPING:

1 cup (250 mL)	plain yoghurt
¼ cup (50 mL)	Chutney

Sauté the onion and garlic in oil in a 2 quart (2 L) Dutch oven. Add the ginger, turmeric and curry powder. Add more oil and rice and sauté for 2 minutes. Add the remaining ingredients other than the apples and topping and simmer for 25 minutes.

Add the apples and simmer for a further 10 minutes or until water is absorbed. Serve, topped with yoghurt and chutney and other garnishes to your liking.

Yield: 8 servings.

GREAT NORTHERN BEAN DISH

A simple, Spanish dish that goes well with meat or sausage.

Ingredients

1½ cups (375 mL)	Great Northern beans
2 Tbsp. (30 mL)	Oil
1	Onion, medium, chopped
1 cup (250 mL)	Tomatoes, canned, chopped
	Salt and pepper (to taste)
¼-½ cup (50-125 mL)	Sherry (optional)
1	Bay leaf, medium
	Parsley, garnish

Cook soaked beans for 2 hours or until tender, drain. Sauté onion in oil until tender. Add the tomatoes, seasoning, sherry and bay leaf. Add liquid (water or reserved bean liquid) to cover. Simmer for 30 minutes. Serve hot, sprinkled with parsley.

Yield: 6 servings.

LAMB AND LENTIL CASSEROLE

Legumes, meat and vegetables; they are all here in one dish, with a very special flavor.

Ingredients

1 cup (250 mL)	Lentils, washed
2 cups (500 mL)	Water
3 Tbsp. (45 mL)	Oil
1½ lb (750 g)	Lamb, lean, boneless, cubed
1 cup (250 mL)	Mushrooms
½ cup (125 mL)	Onion, chopped
1	Garlic clove, diced
1 tsp. (5 mL)	Rosemary, dried
¼ tsp. (1 mL)	Cardamon
1 cup (250 mL)	Tomatoes, canned, chopped
1	Acorn squash, medium (optional)
1 lb (500 g)	Spinach, fresh, frozen or canned
1 Tbsp. (30 mL)	Lemon juice

Brown lamb cubes in oil in a large Dutch oven or heavy casserole, Cook lentils in water for 30 minutes until tender. Drain, put lentils into casserole. Sauté mushrooms, onion and garlic about 3 minutes in drippings. Add to casserole with tomatoes and seasonings. Cover and bake at 375°F (190°C) until lamb begins to get tender, about 45 minutes.

Cut squash into ½ inch (1 cm) slices. Peel and cut each slice into 3 pieces — about 3½ cups (1 L). Add to casserole, cover and bake until meat and squash are tender, about 30 minutes.
Steam spinach until tender, drain, and at the last minute mix into casserole lightly with a fork. Drizzle lemon juice over contents of casserole. Serve.

This dish can be made in a large fry pan.

Yield: 6-8 servings.

LENTIL CHOWDER

Ingredients

4 slices	Bacon, chopped
1 cup (250 mL)	Onion, chopped
1 cup (250 mL)	Celery, chopped
2 Tbsp. (30 mL)	Oil
1½ cups (375 mL)	Lentils, washed
4 cups (1 L)	Water
28 oz (796 mL)	Tomatoes, canned
2 cups (500 mL)	Potatoes, raw, diced
1-2 tsp. (5-10 mL)	Salt
¼ tsp. (1 mL)	Oregano
	Pepper (to taste)
½ Tbsp. (7 mL)	Hickory smoke (optional)

Sauté bacon, onion and celery in oil. Cook all ingredients together in a covered Dutch oven or soup kettle for 45 minutes.

Yield: 8 servings.

LENTIL LOAF

A good, high protein lunch or supper dish.

Ingredients

1 cup (250 mL)	Lentils, washed
3 cups (750 mL)	Water
2 Tbsp. (30 mL)	Butter or margarine
7½ oz (225 g)	Cheese, cheddar, grated
¼ cup (50 mL)	Onion, minced
¼ tsp. (1 mL)	Thyme or savory
¼ tsp. (1 mL)	Salt
1	Egg, beaten
½ cup (125 mL)	Soft bread crumbs
½ cup (125 mL)	Carrots, coarsely grated

Simmer lentils in water until tender about 30 minutes. Drain and mash while hot. Combine with butter, cheese, onion and seasoning. Combine beaten egg, crumbs and carrots and mix with the lentil mixture.

Grease a medium loaf pan and pack the mixture evenly in the pan. Bake until the centre is not wet when tested with a toothpick, about 45 minutes at 350°F (180°C).

Serve with tomato, cheese or mushroom sauce or with sour cream.

Yield: 5 servings.

LENTIL AND PASTA BAKE

Since legume protein and grain protein together meet our protein needs more exactly than either alone, it is fortunate when people around the world over eat locally grown crops. It adds up to a grain and legume cuisine. In the Orient it is soybeans and rice, beans and tortillas in Mexico, beans on toast in England and pocket bread stuffed with legumes in the Middle East. Lentil, pea and bean soups served with a range of bread, buns and flat breads are universal favorites.

This dish is based on an Italian lasagne and makes a good complete protein vegetarian meal, even if no meat is added.

Ingredients

1 cup (250 mL)	Lentils, washed
2 Tbsp. (30 mL)	Oil
1 lb (500 g)	Beef, ground (optional)
2	Garlic cloves, crushed
½ cup (125 mL)	Onion, chopped
14 oz (396 g)	Tomatoes, canned, chopped
2 Tbsp. (30 mL)	Tomato paste
1	Bay leaf, large
1 tsp.	Basil, dried
	Salt (to taste)
	Pepper (to taste)
8 oz. (250 g)	Lasagne noodles
4 Tbsp. (60 mL)	Butter
⅓ cup (75 mL)	Flour
2 cups (500 mL)	Milk
½ cup (125 mL)	Cheese (Cheddar, Mozzarella, or Parmesan, grated)

Cook the lentils for 30 minutes. (See page 13). Drain. Preheat oven to 350°F (180°C). Brown the ground beef if used. Cook onion and garlic gently in oil. Add lentils, beef, tomatoes, tomato paste, bay leaf, basil, salt and pepper. Stir well and simmer gently while preparing the pasta.

Cook the lasagne according to package directions. Make the sauce by heating the butter in a pan, stir in flour and add milk slowly, stirring constantly. Simmer, do not boil. Add cheese.

. . . continued . . .

Arrange the lentil sauce, pasta and cheese sauce in layers in a 9 x 13 inch (23 x 33 cm) pan. Do not have noodles as the first layer on the bottom of the pan. Top with grated cheese. Cover tightly with foil and bake for 45 minutes.

Yield: 6-8 servings.

LENTIL PATTIES

Count on lentils, nuts and yoghurt to complete the protein in these patties.

Ingredients

1 cup (250 mL)	Lentils, washed
2 cups (500 mL)	Water for cooking
½ cup (125 mL)	Onion, finely chopped
¾ cup (175 mL)	Sunflower seeds
1 or 2	Eggs, 1 large or 2 small
⅓ cup (75 mL)	Bread crumbs, dry, fine
¼ cup (50 mL)	Walnuts, chopped
¼ cup (50 mL)	Chili sauce
	Salt (to taste)
	Pepper (to taste)
2 Tbsp. (30 mL)	Margarine or butter
½ cup (125 mL)	Yoghurt, plain

Simmer lentils in water for 30 minutes or until tender. Drain. Sauté onion until clear. Mash lentils, combine all ingredients up to salt and pepper, into 6 patties.

Cook in butter or margarine over medium heat until each side is golden brown and patties are thoroughly heated through. Serve topped with a spoonful of yoghurt.

Yield: 6 servings.

LENTIL-POTATO CAKES

Serve with bacon as a lunch or supper dish or serve as a side dish with meat.

Ingredients

1 cup (250 mL)	Lentils
3	Potatoes, medium, cooked, mashed
1 Tbsp. (15 mL)	Lemon juice
2 Tbsp. (30 mL)	Margarine or butter, melted
	Salt and pepper (to taste)
	Flour
	Bacon fat

Cook the lentils for 30 minutes. (See page 13). Drain well and mash. Combine the thoroughly mashed potatoes and lentils. Blend well. Stir in the lemon juice, melted butter and salt and pepper. Form into flat, round cakes and flour them all around. Cook in hot bacon fat.

Yield: 6 servings.

LENTIL AND RICE RING

Good to look at, good to eat, served with Chicken-Lentil Curry. (See page 54).

Ingredients

1 cup (250 mL)	Lentils, washed
2/3 cup (150 mL)	Onion, mild, chopped
1/4 cup (50 mL)	Almonds, slivered
1/4 cup (50 mL)	Oil
6 cups (1.5 L)	Rice, long-grain, cooked
1/2 cup (125 mL)	Raisins, light

Cook lentils 30 minutes. (See page 13). Drain. Sauté onions and almonds in oil until lightly browned, stirring a few minutes. Add lentil mixture to hot rice and raisins. Press lightly into a 6 cup (1.5 L) ring mold.

Unmold and fill with chicken lentil curry. Top with chopped peanuts and shredded coconut and more raisins. Garnish with parsley.

Yield: 6 servings.

LENTIL-SAUSAGE CASSEROLE

This easy to make lentil-sausage casserole is a fine combination of legumes, vegetables and meat. It rated a high score when tested by the professional taste-testing panel.

Ingredients

1 cup (250 mL)	Lentils
2 cups (500 mL)	Water
¾ lb (375 g)	Sausage meat, slice and fry
⅓ cup (75 mL)	Flour
	Garlic powder (to taste)
2 cups (500 mL)	Tomatoes, canned
½ cup (125 mL)	Onions, chopped, sautéed
	Mozzarella cheese, shredded

Cook lentils in water for 30 minutes and drain. Brown sausage and pour off excess fat. Stir in flour and garlic powder to the sausage. Add tomatoes and sautéed onions. Combine the entire mixture with the lentils and bake in a shallow baking dish.

Top the mixture with a generous sprinkling of mozzarella cheese and bake for 30 minutes in a 350°F (180°C) oven until hot and bubbly.

Yield: 4 servings.

LENTIL TACO FILLING

STEP ONE: Sauce of Lentils and Green Chilies.

Ingredients

2 Tbsp. (30 mL)	Butter or margarine
½ cup (125 mL)	Onion, minced
1	Garlic clove, crushed
1½ cups (375 mL)	Tomatoes, canned, chopped, drained
2 oz. (55 g)	Green chilies, canned (not pickled)
½ tsp. (2 mL)	Salt
1½ cups (375 mL)	Lentils, cooked, drained

In heavy skillet cook onion and garlic until tender, but not browned. Stir in tomatoes and salt, simmer over low heat. Rinse and scrape seeds and the membrane from the green chili pepper. Chop and add chilies and cooked lentils to the sauce. **Caution:** always wash hands with soap and water after handling chilies. This chili pepper rubbed into the eyes can be painful. Keep mixture warm or reheat before adding second sauce just before serving.

STEP TWO: Cheese Sauce

2 Tbsp. (30 mL)	Butter or margarine
2 Tbsp. (30 mL)	Flour
½ tsp. (2 mL)	Salt
1 cup (250 mL)	Light cream
½ lb (250 g)	Cheese, mild cheddar or Monterey Jack

In a heavy sauce pan, melt butter. Stir in flour. Cook over low heat for several minutes. Remove from heat. Carefully stir in cream. Cook sauce gently, stirring constantly until thickened. Add this sauce, while hot to the heated lentil-chili mixture. Mix lightly, keeping covered, over low heat. About 3 or 4 minutes before serving, stir in the finely diced cheese and heat until melted. Keep hot over a food warmer. Garnish with shredded lettuce, tomato, olives and red or green pepper strips.

Yield: 4 generous cups to use as a taco filling.

LENTIL ZUCCHINI CHEESE BAKE

Serve with a green salad and brown buns.

Ingredients

1 cup (250 mL)	Lentils, washed
2 Tbsp. (9 mL)	Oil
⅓ cup (75 mL)	Onion, finely chopped
1 cup (250 mL)	Celery, finely chopped
1	Garlic clove, minced
1 tsp. (5 mL)	Salt
1 tsp. (5 mL)	Oregano
14 oz (398 mL)	Tomatoes, canned, chopped with juice
5½ oz (156 mL)	Tomato paste, canned
4	Zucchini, medium
2	Eggs, beaten
½ cup (125 mL)	Flour
⅓ cup (75 mL)	Oil
8 oz (250 g)	Cheese slices or mozzarella cheese, grated

Cook lentils 30 minutes or until tender. (See page 13). Drain. Sauté onion, celery and garlic in oil. Add salt, oregano, tomatoes and tomato paste and simmer (without lentils) for 30 minutes.

Cut zucchini unpeeled in ½ inch (1 cm) slices, dip in egg, then in flour. Heat oil in a large skillet at medium heat. Brown zucchini slices on both sides, drain on paper towelling.

Place a layer of zucchini slices in a 10 x 6 x 3 inch (25 x 12 cm) baking dish. Top with half the tomato sauce and half the cheese. Spread the lentils on top of that and repeat the cheese and tomato sauce layer, ending with a topping of cheese. Bake uncovered at 400°F (200°C) for 15-20 minutes.

Yield: 8-10 servings.

MIDDLE EAST SPICY LENTIL FRITTERS

Ingredients

1½ cups (375 mL)	Lentils, washed
3 cups (750 mL)	Water
2 Tbsp. (30 mL)	Butter or margarine
1	Onion, medium, grated
1½ tsp. (3 mL)	Cumin
1½ tsp. (3 mL)	Coriander
1 Tbsp. (15 mL)	Parsley, chopped, fresh
1 tsp. (2 mL)	Salt
	Black pepper, freshly ground (to taste)
1	Egg
	Oil for pan frying

Simmer the lentils in water for 30 minutes or until soft. Mash or blend the lentils with the butter, add the onion, spices and egg. Mix thoroughly. Chill the mixture for 1 hour.

Form the mixture into small cakes on a lightly floured board. Fry the cakes in hot, shallow oil, drain on paper towels.

Serve with small buns or pita bread and a green salad for a tasty lunch. Suggested toppings — yoghurt, chutney, mayonnaise.

Yield: 4-6 servings.

MIXED BEAN CHOWDER

This makes a substantial meal and demonstrates how to use beans interchangeably.

Ingredients

¾ cup (175 mL)	Great Northern dried beans
¾ cup (175 mL)	Dried pink or pinto beans
4 cups (1 L)	Water for soaking
2 Tbsp. (30 mL)	Butter or margarine
1 cup (250 mL)	Onion, chopped
1	Garlic clove, minced
1	Potato, diced, medium, cooked
½ cup (125 mL)	Green pepper, diced
1½ tsp. (7 mL)	Salt
½ tsp. (2 mL)	Pepper
½-1 cup (125-250 mL)	Milk, whole

Sort and soak beans; use quick soak method page 13. Drain beans; discard soak water. In a large pot combine soaked beans and 4 cups (1 L) fresh water. In a small skillet, sauté onion and garlic in butter or margarine until almost tender but not brown. Add potatoes. Add to beans. Bring to a boil. Reduce heat. Cover and simmer until beans are almost tender.

Remove 1 cup of bean-potato mixture. Mash in a small bowl with a fork or potato masher. Return mashed mixture to chowder and stir well. Add green pepper, salt and pepper and enough milk to obtain desired consistency. Cook slowly 10 minutes, stirring occasionally, to prevent scorching.

Yield: 6 servings.

REFRIED BEANS

Ingredients

2 cups (500 mL)	Dried Beans, cooked, drained
¼ cup (50 mL)	Onions, chopped
⅛ tsp. (½ mL)	Hot pepper sauce
⅛ tsp. (½ mL)	Garlic powder
¼ tsp. (1 mL)	Chili powder
½ cup (125 mL)	Bacon fat for frying
	Cheese, old, cheddar type
½ cup (125 mL)	shredded

Mash beans thoroughly. Combine with onions, pepper sauce, garlic powder and chili powder and mix. Heat bacon fat in frying pan over moderate heat and add bean mixture. Cook until edges are crisp and brown. Sprinkle with cheese and leave on heat until cheese melts. Serve hot.

Yield: 4-6 servings.

SWEET AND SOUR LENTILS AND RICE

There is a nutritionally sound, scientific reason for combining legumes and cereals to make a complete protein. Legumes are low in the amino acid methionine and high in the amino acid lysine, thus complementing cereal proteins which are high in methionine and low in lysine. For this reason, a combination of legumes and cereal proteins provide good amino acid balance in our diets. Good combinations are rice and lentils, beans and barley, lentils and corn, lentils and wheat.

Ingredients

1 cup (250 mL)	Rice long-grain, brown or white
⅓ cup (75 mL)	Lentils, washed
2½ cups (375 mL)	Water
½ tsp. (2 mL)	Salt

SAUCE:

½ cup (125 mL)	Vinegar, white
½ cup (125 mL)	Sugar, brown
3 Tbsp. (45 mL)	Soy sauce
4 Tbsp. (60 mL)	Catsup
1½ cups (375 mL)	Pineapple juice or water
3 Tbsp. (45 mL)	Cornstarch

Combine rice and lentils in water. Bring to the boil, reduce heat to simmer and cook for 25 minutes or until rice and lentils are tender.

Stir together the other ingredients except the cornstarch, heat. Mix the cornstarch with a little cold water, add some hot mixture and then add to the sauce. Stir until thickened, pour sauce over rice and lentils and serve.

VARIATIONS

Add ½ lb. (250 g) cooked sliced sausage to rice and lentils prior to sauce.
Add heated, diced pork or chicken.
Add sauce to cooked meat and serve rice and lentils as a side dish.
Add ½ cup (125 mL) diced, cooked, mild onion.

. . . continued . . .

The sauce is delicious with pork button bones or diced pork with green pepper and pineapple chunks.

Yield: 6 servings.

SAUCY LENTILS

A good luncheon or supper dish served with buns and salad or as a side dish.

Ingredients

1½ cups (375 mL)	Lentils, washed
3 cups (750 mL)	Water
1	Onion, medium chopped
1 Tbsp. (15 mL)	Butter
2 stalks (2 stalks)	Celery, diced
1 can, 10 oz (284 mL)	Mushroom soup
½ cup (125 mL)	Sour cream
1 tsp. (5 mL)	Worcestershire sauce

Simmer washed lentils in water for 25 minutes or until done. Drain.

Sauté onion and celery in butter. Heat mushroom soup, add lentils, onion, celery, worcestershire sauce and sour cream. Heat through and serve immediately.

NOTE: Fresh or canned mushrooms may be added.

Yield: 6 servings.

LENTIL PIZZA

This pizza was served to two eleven year old boys for a film documentary featuring legumes. They are shown delightedly eating lentil sausage pizza and lentil sprout salad.

Pizza makes a very good vegetarian meal — just leave out the sausage. It is filling, tasty, looks good and smells wonderful with the aroma of homemade bread.

If you have a favorite French bread recipe it will make a good base. A simple way is to buy a frozen pizza shell, and fill. Otherwise, there are many dough variations, one of which is:

Ingredients

1 package	Fresh or dry-active yeast
½ cup (125 mL)	Water, warm to dissolve yeast
½ tsp. (2 mL)	Sugar, in yeast water
	Flour, whole wheat or all
2½ cups (625 mL)	purpose
½ tsp. (2 mL)	Salt
3 Tbsp. (45 mL)	Oil, margarine or butter
1	Egg, beaten

Mix yeast, sugar and warm water in a bowl — set aside for 10 minutes to ferment. Mix the flour and salt, add the shortening and rub in with your hands. Add the beaten egg and yeast, mixing with hands to make a dough. It should be soft enough to knead, but firm and pliable. Adjust consistency if necessary by adding a little water or flour.

Knead on a floured board for about 5 minutes. Place in a greased bowl, cover, set in a warm place to rise until more than double in bulk, about 1½ hours. Punch down, cover, let rise again. Cut dough in half and roll each into two 12 inch (30 cm) circles. Place on two 12 inch (30 cm) greased pizza pans, turning edges of dough up slightly. Brush each circle with oil.

. . . continued . . .

TOPPING

Ingredients

2 cups (500 mL)	Lentils, cooked
1 lb (500 g)	Sausage, bulk (optional)
3 cups (750 mL)	Tomato sauce
¾ tsp. (3 mL)	Garlic powder
1 tsp. (5 mL)	Oregano
1 tsp. (5 mL)	Basil
½ tsp. (2 mL)	Thyme
3 cups (750 mL)	Cheese mixture: sharp cheddar, Swiss, mozzarella
1 cup (250 mL)	Mushrooms, fresh, sliced Cheese topping: grated parmesan or mozzarella

Cook lentils, drain. Cook sausage, if used, pour off excess fat leaving enough to "oil" lentils lightly. Add broken up sausage to lentils and mix thoroughly.

Combine tomato sauce with seasonings. Spread half of sauce over each pizza. Add sausage and lentil mix and mixture of grated cheeses. Top with mushrooms, sprinkle with grated Parmesan or mozzarella cheese. Preheat oven to 400°F (200°C) and bake for 15-20 minutes until the edges are puffed and golden brown.

Pizza freezes well if prepared in advance. Place the uncooked pizza in the freezer, wrapped in foil. To use, defrost for 20-30 minutes while the oven heats and bake as usual.

Varying the variety of cheese is your privilege.

HONEYED BEANS

Good with pork or sausage dishes or served alone with fresh brown bread and a green salad.

Ingredients

1½ cups (375 mL)	Pinto beans
1	Onion, mild, medium, finely chopped
2 Tbsp. (30 mL)	Oil
¼ cup (50 mL)	Honey
1 or 2	Garlic clove crushed
	Salt and pepper (to taste)

Cook pre-soaked beans in water for 1-2 hours. Drain. Sauté onion in oil until tender. Add onion, honey, garlic and seasoning to beans. Bake at 400°F (200°C) for 30 minutes in a covered casserole. Add more water if the beans become dry.

Yield: 6 servings.

SIDE·DISHES

Most people like something new and different. These recipes for side-dishes are to be used like vegetables, served to accompany a main dish. They are fairly simple ideas for enhancing the meal with a nutritious menu change.

Some are hearty enough and good enough to serve as a main dish. They are easily adapted to the food likes of the individual or family. For instance the "Lentils and Rice" dish (page 80) may be transformed into an East Indian dish by adding curry powder, cumin seed and lemon juice, served with mango, chutney and a curry sauce. The English version of this lentil and rice combination is known as "Kedgeree" and the East Indian as "Khitchari", a spicy mixture, ideal for vegetarians.

CURRIED LENTILS

For the curry lover this is an excellent accompaniment for chicken or fish.

Ingredients

1 cup (250 mL)	Lentils
2 cups (500 mL)	Water
2 Tbsp. (30 mL)	Butter
1 cup (250 mL)	Onion, chopped, mild
½ cup (125 mL)	Celery, diced
1-3 tsp. (5-15 mL)	Curry powder
¼ cup (50 mL)	Water
1 Tbsp. (15 mL)	Flour
¼ cup (50 mL)	Wine, dry, white
1 tsp. (5 mL)	Salt
	Pepper, freshly ground (to taste)

Cook lentils in water for 30 minutes. Drain. Melt butter in skillet. Add onion, celery, curry powder to taste and ¼ cup (50 mL) water. Cover and simmer for 10 minutes.

Mix flour with wine, blend well and add to skillet. Add lentils, pepper and salt. Simmer for 15 minutes.

Yield: 6 servings.

GREEK STYLE LENTILS

Ingredients

1 cup (250 mL)	Lentils
2 cups (500 mL)	Water for cooking
1 cup (250 mL)	Onions, chopped, sautéed
1	Garlic clove
1	Bay leaf, large
2 Tbsp. (30 mL)	Olive oil
3-4	Anise seeds
	Wine vinegar, few drops

Boil lentils and discard first water. Add more water, bring to a boil again and simmer until lentils are tender. Add onions, garlic, bay leaves, olive oil and anise seeds. Top with a few drops of vinegar.

Yield: 4 servings.

LENTIL BARLEY STEW

Ingredients

¼ cup (50 mL)	Butter or margarine
¾ cup (175 mL)	Celery, chopped
¾ cup (175 mL)	Onion, chopped
6 cups (1.5 L)	Water
¾ cup (175 mL)	Lentils, washed
¾ cup (175 mL)	Barley or brown rice
½ tsp. (2 mL)	Rosemary
½ tsp. (2 mL)	Garlic salt
1 tsp. (5 mL)	Salt
¼ tsp. (1 mL)	Pepper
28 oz (796 mL)	Tomatoes, canned
½ cup (125 mL)	Carrots, shredded

Sauté onion and celery in butter. Add water and lentils, cook for 20 minutes. Add other ingredients except carrots. Simmer for 45 minutes. Add carrots, cook 5 minutes and serve.

Yield: 8 servings.

LENTILS AND GREEN ONIONS

Serve with roast meat; this is especially good with lamb. Add a little of the drippings from the meat to the lentils so they match the flavor of the meat.

Ingredients

1	Onion, small, finely chopped
1 Tbsp. (15 mL)	Butter or margarine
1½ cups (375 mL)	Lentils
1	Bay leaf
3 cups (750 mL)	Water
4	Green onions, tops, chopped
	Salt and pepper (to taste)

Cook the onion in butter until clear, then stir in lentils, bay leaf, salt and pepper. Cover with water and bring to a boil. Simmer for 30 minutes or until the lentils are tender and the liquid absorbed.

Stir in the green onions and some hot drippings or gravy from the meat. Add salt and pepper to taste. Serve hot.

Yield: 6-8 servings.

LENTIL PILAF

Ingredients

1 cup (250 mL)	Lentils
1	Onion, medium, chopped
¼ cup (50 mL)	Butter or margarine
1 cup (250 mL)	Mushrooms, canned or fresh
2 cups (500 mL)	Water, boiling
1 cube	Chicken bouillon

Combine all ingredients, cover and simmer for 40-50 minutes or put in a casserole, cover and bake at 350°F (180°C) for 1 hour. Check and add liquid if necessary. This is also good using equal parts of lentils and pearl barley.

Yield: 6 servings.

LENTILS AND PRUNES

This simple dish is good served as a side-dish with a rich meat, like pork.

Ingredients

1 cup (250 mL)	Lentils, washed
	Prunes, halves, stoned and
1 cup (250 mL)	soaked overnight
¼ cup (50 mL)	Sherry, dry
½ tsp. (2 mL)	Salt
1 Tbsp. (15 mL)	Lemon juice

Cook the prunes and lentils together in the prune soaking liquid for approximately 1 hour. Drain, add salt, sherry and lemon juice. Serve hot.

Yield: 4-6 servings.

LENTILS AND RICE

Serve this with meat and/or vegetables.

Ingredients

1 cup (250 mL)	Lentils
2 cups (500 mL)	Water
1	Onion, large, mild, chopped
1	Garlic clove, chopped
1 Tbsp. (15 mL)	Oil
½ cup (125 mL)	Long-grain rice
2	Tomatoes, large, ripe
1¼ cups (300 mL)	Vegetable or chicken broth
	Salt and pepper (to taste)

Simmer the lentils for 15 minutes in water. Drain. Sauté the onions and garlic in the oil. Add the rice and stir for 3 minutes. Add the lentils, tomatoes and broth. Season, bring to the boil, lower the heat, cover and cook for 25 minutes or until lentils and rice are tender.

Yield: 6 servings.

PEASE PUDDING

"Pease pudding hot, pease pudding cold, pease pudding in the pot, nine days old." Today pease pudding has become more a memory of our childhood nursery rhymes than an item in the daily diet.

Traditionally a British recipe, boiled in a "pudding cloth" and served with boiled beef. A classic English cookbook, "Mrs. Beeton's Cookery" describes it as "an exceedingly nice accompaniment to boiled beef".

This is a good side dish for roast beef, pork or lamb with crisp browned potatoes, broccoli, lots of gravy and applesauce or mint sauce. It is simple to make, high in fibre, low in fat and cholesterol.

Ingredients

1 cup (250 mL)	Split peas, yellow or green
1	Onion, large, diced
3 Tbsp. (45 mL)	Butter or margarine
	Salt and pepper (to taste)

. . . continued . . .

Cover the split peas with water and simmer gently until tender —
about 30-45 minutes. Drain. Sauté onion in margarine until soft about
10 minutes. Add onion to cooked split peas. Serve hot.

Variations: Grated lemon rind, or marjoram or cumin or caraway or
fennel seeds are good additions. Add to the onion when it is nearly
cooked.

Yield: 4 servings.

LENTILS, RICE AND BARLEY-PEAS'N

The mixing of legumes with cereals has been practiced throughout the
ages. When the Romans ate barley it was usually eaten in combination
with lentils, beans or other plant foods. In Medieval England bread
was made with beans and peas added to various cereals.

This recipe was sent to me with the information that "it's an adaptation
of an old Polish-Jewish dish my mother used to feed us when we were
kids, called 'peas'n".

Ingredients

1 cup (250 mL)	Lentils, dry peas or dry beans
1 cup (250 mL)	Pearl barley
1 cup (250 mL)	Rice, brown
6 cups (1.5 L)	Water
1	Onion, mild, large, chopped
	Mushrooms, sliced, fresh or
1 lb (500 g)	canned
½ tsp. (2 mL)	Salt
3 cups (750 mL)	Chicken or beef stock

Combine the lentils, barley and rice (or beans/peas) and bring to a boil
in the 6 cups of water. Cover and simmer for about 30 minutes or until
tender and the water soaked up. Drain and rinse well in a collander.

Sauté the onion and add mushrooms, salt and stock. Place all ingredients in a covered casserole and bake in a 350°F (180°C) oven for 30
minutes. Serve as a side dish instead of potatoes.

Yield: 10-12 servings.

LENTILS AS A VEGETABLE I

Prepare these lentils as vegetables the same way that you would prepare potatoes. Simply cook them until tender and serve with salt, pepper and butter.

Ingredients

1½ cups (375 mL)	Lentils, washed
3 cups (750 mL)	Water
	Salt and pepper
	Butter

Cook lentils in water until tender — about 30 minutes. Add salt, pepper and butter, to taste.

Yield: 6 servings.

LENTILS AS A VEGETABLE II

Ingredients

2½ cups (625 mL)	Lentils
5 cups (1.25 L)	Water
1	Garlic clove, minced
1	Onion, whole
2	Cloves, whole
1	Carrot, chopped
½ tsp. (2 mL)	Savor
½ tsp. (2 mL)	Basil
	Butter
	Lemon juice

Add all ingredients except butter and lemon juice to the lentils and water. Simmer for 30 minutes or until lentils and vegetables are cooked. Drain, remove cloves and serve hot with butter and lemon juice added.

Yield: 8 servings.

WEIGHT·WATCHERS

As they are low in cholesterol and sodium, non-sweet and high in fibre, legumes are excellent for Weight Watchers diets. The following recipes are printed by kind permission of Weight Watchers International.

AUSTRIAN LENTIL SALAD

(Linsen salat)

Ingredients

8 oz (250 g)	Lentils, cooked
2 oz (50 mL)	Scallion, finely chopped
2 tsp. (10 mL)	Vegetable oil
2 tsp. (10 mL)	Vinegar
	Salt and pepper (to taste)
¼ tsp. (1 mL)	Savory

Combine ingredients, mix well, chill until ready to use.

Yield: 1 serving

LENTILS WITH RICE

Ingredients

1 cup (250 mL)	Chicken bouillon
1 cup (250 mL)	Celery, sliced
⅓ cup (75 mL)	Carrots, sliced
8 oz (250 g)	Lentils, cooked
1 tsp. (5 mL)	Chives, chopped
1 tsp. (5 mL)	Diet margarine
1 tsp. (5 mL)	Sage, chopped, fresh
	Salt and pepper (to taste)
½ cup (125 mL)	Cooked, enriched rice

In saucepan, combine chicken bouillon, celery and carrots and cook until vegetables are soft — 15 to 20 minutes.

Remove from heat, stir in remaining ingredients, mix well and serve hot as main dish.

Yield: 1 serving.

BLACK BEAN SALAD

This bean salad includes ingredients to give a typical and traditional Spanish flavor, but modified to fit Weight Watchers Food Program.

Ingredients

4 oz (125 mL)	Onion, diced
4	Green peppers, medium, chopped
2	Garlic cloves, mashed
1½ lbs (750 g)	Dried black beans, cooked (see note)
1 cup (250 mL)	Beef bouillon
	Oregano (dash)
	Brandy extract (dash)
¼ cup (50 mL)	Vegetable oil
¼ cup (50 mL)	Wine vinegar
¾ tsp. (3 mL)	Mustard, prepared
	Salt and pepper (to taste)

In a preheated non-stick saucepan, lightly brown onion, green pepper and garlic. Add the beans, bouillon, oregano and brandy extract. Simmer for 45 minutes. Cool.

Combine oil, wine vinegar, mustard, salt and pepper. Pour over beans, chill until ready to serve.

NOTE: To cook dried beans: Cover 1½ cups (325 mL) dried black beans with 4½ cups (1 L) water. Let soak overnight. Cook about 2-2½ hours or until beans are soft. Weigh serving.

Yield: 4 servings.

BLACK BEAN AND RICE STEW
(Feijoada)

Black beans are a staple of the Brazilian diet. The use of garlic, onion, tomatoes and hot red peppers in this recipe is of Iberian origin.

Ingredients

1	Green pepper, medium, diced
1	Garlic clove, small, crushed
½ tsp. (2 mL)	Oregano
¼ tsp. (1 mL)	Cumin
¼ cup (50 mL)	Beef bouillon
	Dried black beans, cooked
1 cup (250 mL)	(See page 13)
½ cup (125 mL)	Brown rice, cooked
1 oz (30 mL)	Onion, red, sliced

In a saucepan combine green pepper, garlic, oregano and cumin with ¼ cup (50 mL) beef bouillon. Simmer 10 minutes; stir in black beans and rice and more bouillon if desired. Serve in bowl with slices of raw onion.

Yield: 1 serving.

LENTIL SOUP
(Faki)

This soup, sharpened with vinegar can be made ahead of time and refrigerated for several days as it improves with age. It also freezes well.

Ingredients

1 qt (1.25 L)	Beef bouillon
1 lb 2 oz (560 g)	Lentils, cooked
	Salt and pepper (to taste)
6 Tbsp. (90 mL)	Tomato purée
3 oz (90 mL)	Onion, finely chopped
¼ cup (50 mL)	Carrot, finely chopped
½ rib	Celery, finely chopped
½ clove	Garlic, minced or pressed
1 Tbsp. (15 mL)	Vinegar or lemon juice

Combine bouillon, lentils, salt and pepper in a large saucepan. Bring to a boil. Add remaining ingredients except vinegar. Return mixture to a boil; reduce heat and simmer for at least 30 minutes or until vegetables are tender.

Divide into 3 soup bowls, stir 1 tsp. (5 mL) of vinegar or lemon juice into each bowl of soup as it is served.

Yield: 3 servings.

HEARTY BEAN AND VEGETABLE SOUP

Caldogallego, a traditional Spanish dish to warm the hearts of weight watchers.

Ingredients

2 cups (500 mL)	Beef bouillon
	Dried white beans, cooked or
12 oz (375 mL)	canned white cannellini
4 oz (125 mL)	Beef cooked, cut in strips
3 oz (90 mL)	Ham cooked, cut in strips
1 cup (250 mL)	Turnips, peeled, cubed
2 cups (500 mL)	Cabbage, shredded
2 Tbsp. (30 mL)	Onion, dehydrated
1	Garlic clove, peeled, minced
	Salt and freshly ground pepper
	(to taste)

Combine all ingredients in a 2 quart (2 L) saucepan, and bring to a boil. Cover and simmer gently until turnips are tender, 15 to 20 minutes. Divide evenly and serve.

Yield: 4 servings.

LENTIL AND SPINACH SOUP

A Middle Eastern hot pot.

Ingredients

12 oz (375 mL)	Lentils, fresh cooked (reserve liquid
3 cups (750 mL)	Lentil liquid, plus water
1½ cups (375 mL)	Spinach, frozen, chopped, thawed and well drained
3 packets	Instant beef broth and seasoning mix
3 oz (100 mL)	Onion, sliced
	Pepper, freshly ground (to taste)
1 Tbsp. (15 mL)	Lemon juice

In a large sauce pan, combine lentils, liquid, spinach, broth mix and onion. Cover and simmer 20 minutes. Stir in lemon juice and serve hot with sprinkling of pepper.

Yield: 3 servings.

PASTA AND LENTILS

A favorite Italian pasta dish, designed for one.

Ingredients

8 oz (250 mL)	Green Lentils, cooked, drained
1 cup (250 mL)	Water
⅓ cup (75 mL)	Carrots, chopped
⅓ cup (75 mL)	Celery, chopped
2 oz (60 mL)	Onion, chopped
1	Tomato, peeled, chopped
1 package	Instant beef broth and seasoning mix
1	Bay leaf, small
1	Garlic clove, minced
½ tsp. (2 mL)	Salt
⅛ tsp. (05 mL)	Pepper
1 Tbsp. (15 mL)	Margarine
⅔ cup (150 mL)	Macaroni, cooked, enriched

In medium saucepan combine all ingredients except macaroni and margarine. Bring to a boil; reduce heat; cover and cook 40 minutes. Remove bay leaf. Stir in macaroni, heat. Remove from heat; stir in margarine.

Yield: 1 serving.

SPLIT PEA SOUP

This East Indian "Dal" features curry powder and hot green chili peppers.

Ingredients

12 oz (375 mL)	Split peas, yellow, cooked, drained (Reserve liquid)
4 cups (1 L)	Liquid — water plus reserved liquid (see note)
1 cup (250 mL)	Celery, diced
1 Tbsp. (15 mL)	Curry powder
1 Tbsp. (15 mL)	Onion flakes, dehydrated
1 tsp. (5 mL)	Salt
2	Chili peppers, chopped hot green or to taste
1	Bay leaf
	Parsley, chopped

Combine all ingredients in saucepan (except parsley) and bring to a boil. Reduce heat and simmer 45 minutes. Purée in blender container and serve in bowls. Garnish with parsley.

COOKING NOTE: Cover 1 pound (500 g) washed uncooked dried split peas with water; bring to boil, cover pan and simmer gently until peas are tender but still firm. Drain peas (reserve liquid), weigh peas. Freeze serving portion in liquid to cover. Label net weight.

Yield: 4 servings.

GARDEN PEA (plant, pea, pod)

NAVY BEAN SOUP

A hearty soup that, as result of an official U.S. Senate resolution, is served daily in the Senate Dining Room.

Ingredients

4 oz (125 mL)	Navy beans, cooked, dried, drained, reserving liquid
	Water
¼ cup (50 mL)	Celery, diced
¼ cup (50 mL)	Carrots, cooked, diced
1 oz (30 mL)	Onion, chopped
¼ tsp. (1 mL)	Garlic powder
	Bay leaf, small
2 oz (55 g)	Ham, cooked, finely chopped
	Salt and pepper (to taste)
	Cloves, ground (to taste)

In a medium sauce pan, combine liquid from cooked beans and enough water to make 1½ cups (375 mL). Add celery, carrots, onions, garlic and bay leaf. Simmer 15 minutes or until vegetables are tender. Remove bay leaf. Add beans and ham. Heat through. Season with salt, pepper and cloves to taste.

Yield: 1 serving.

SALADS

Lentils for salads should be cooked until tender but not mushy. Bring washed lentils to the boil and simmer for 10-30 minutes.

When cooked they should stand for at least an hour in a dressing with a good amount of vinegar or lemon juice. Mustard gives a good, zesty flavor to lentil salads. Keep cooked lentils in the refrigerator; bring them out and add raw vegetables and herbs. Mix with a small amount of rice or croutons if desired. Garnish and serve as a salad-cum-main-dish.

Bean and lentil salads are delicious as a **main course.** They should be seasoned and dressed while still hot. If you are using canned beans or lentils, reheat them before dressing. Toss them with a nippy garlic and mustard dressing laced with your favorite fresh herbs. Good additions are onions, tomatoes, green peppers, raw cauliflower florets, tuna fish or olives. Serve these salads with lettuce and a garnish of hard boiled eggs.

NIPPY DRESSING

Ingredients

1	Garlic clove, crushed
	Salt and pepper (to taste)
1 Tbsp. (15 mL)	Lemon juice
1 Tbsp. (15 mL)	Wine vinegar
1/2 tsp. (2 mL)	Mustard, dry
2/3 cup (150 mL)	Salad oil or olive oil, best quality

Crush the garlic, add salt and pepper. Add lemon juice, wine vinegar and mustard. Add oil and shake to blend in a jar or whisk in a bowl with a wire whisk. This may be done with the oil added all at once or in stages. Whisk in desired herbs, taste. Correct seasonings. Whisk in more seasonings, oil or vinegar as needed.

Yield: 2/3 cup of dressing.

BEAN SALAD

White, black, pinto, pink, kidney beans or lentils are all equally good to make a delicious, hearty salad. Cook the beans until soft but not mushy. Dress and season them while still warm. If you use canned beans, heat them before dressing and then chill. Use the Nippy Dressing above or your favorite zesty dressing. This is a chance to use garlic and fresh herbs to advantage.

Add: **Green pepper rings**
White or red onion rings
Fresh herbs
Celery
Tomatoes

Garnish: Serve in a lettuce lined bowl and garnish with hard boiled eggs, olives, tomatoes and parsley.

GREEN SALAD WITH LENTIL SPROUTS

Ingredients

2 cups (500 mL)	Lettuce, torn
2 cups (500 mL)	Spinach, torn
2/3 cup (150 mL)	Lentil sprouts
1/2 cup (125 mL)	Red or green pepper, sliced
1 Tbsp. (15 mL)	Green onion, chopped
	Creamy cucumber dressing to moisten

Wash and drain lettuce and spinach. Toss together lettuce, celery, sprouts, red pepper and green onion. Dress with creamy cucumber dressing. Garnish.

NOTE: See page 105 for sprouting your own lentils.

TUNA LENTIL SALAD

Ingredients

1 cup (250 mL)	Green lentils
2 cups (500 mL)	Water
6 oz (170 g)	Tuna, drained
1/3 cup (75 mL)	Mayonnaise
1 Tbsp. (15 mL)	Vinegar
2 tsp. (10 mL)	Sugar
1 cup (250 mL)	Celery, chopped
2 Tbsp. (30 mL)	Onion, mild, chopped
	Garnish

Cook green lentils in water. Drain and chill.

Put all ingredients in a bowl and mix. Garnish with pimento, tomato, green pepper, or chopped green onion tops. Serve in lettuce cups.

Yield: 6 servings.

LEMON LENTIL SALAD MOLD

Serve this main-dish salad with whole grain rolls and a beverage. Use your imagination and have fun with the topping.

Ingredients

1 cup (250 mL)	Green lentils, cooked
3 oz (85 g)	Lemon jelly powder
1½ cups (375 mL)	Boiling water
	Pineapple chunks or crushed,
1 cup (250 mL)	drained
1 cup (250 mL)	Cheddar type cheese, grated
	Whipped cream or topping,
1 cup (250 mL)	sweetened

TOPPING:

1 cup (250 mL)	Celery, diced
1 cup (250 mL)	Green pepper, diced
	Green onion with tops,
1	chopped
½ cup (125 mL)	Mayonnaise
1 cup (250 mL)	Cauliflower florets

May use diced cucumber, shredded carrots or fresh green peas on top.

Cook lentils, drain and cool. Dissolve jelly powder in boiling water. Cool until it starts to set. Add pineapple, cheese and cream or white topping mix. Pour into mold until set.

Mix lentils with celery, green pepper, cauliflower, onions and mayonnaise. Spread over set jelly mixture, chill. Garnish and serve on lettuce or salad greens.

Yield: 8 servings.

LENTIL CRANBERRY MOLD

Good with turkey or chicken or substantial enough for a light lunch if served with cheese and rolls.

Ingredients

½ cup (125 mL)	Green lentils
1 cup (250 mL)	Water
4 cups (1 L)	Cranberries
½ cup (125 mL)	Water
1 cup (250 mL)	Sugar
3 oz (85 g)	Strawberry jelly powder
1 cup (250 mL)	Boiling water
1 cup (250 mL)	Celery, diced
1 cup (250 mL)	Apple, diced
	Lettuce

Cook lentils about 30 minutes until tender. Drain and cool. Cook cranberries in water at a simmer until skins pop. Add sugar and cook for 3 minutes.

Dissolve jelly powder in boiling water stirring well. Chill until it starts to set. Fold in lentils, cranberries, celery and apple. Pour into a 2 quart (2 L) mold or individual molds. Unmold on lettuce. Garnish. Serve with your favorite dressing or creamy cucumber.

Yield: 8 servings.

LENTIL SALAD

This is a decorative salad and makes a fine summer meal served with bread and fresh fruit.

Ingredients

1 cup (250 mL)	Green lentils
2 cups (500 mL)	Water
½ cup (125 mL)	Salad oil
2 Tbsp. (30 mL)	Wine vinegar
1 Tbsp. (15 mL)	French mustard
	Salt and pepper (to taste)
3	Tomatoes, chopped
1	Green or red pepper, seeded or sliced into rings
3	Eggs, hard cooked, sliced
1 Tbsp. (15 mL)	Parsley, for garnish

Cook the lentils in unsalted water for 20-30 minutes until tender but not mushy. Drain while still hot, mix with the oil, vinegar and mustard. Add salt and pepper to taste. Cool, stir the vegetables gently into the salad.

Decorate with sliced eggs and parsley. You may add cauliflower and other raw vegetables and herbs to your liking.

Yield: 4 servings.

MEXICAN RED BEAN SALAD

The bean and rice combination in this salad completes the protein. The salami is an added bonus.

Ingredients

2 cups (500 mL)	Mexican Red Beans, cooked
1 cup (250 mL)	Rice, uncooked
2 cups (500 mL)	Water to cook rice
1 tsp. (5 mL)	Salt
	Pepper (to taste)
²/₃ cup (150 mL)	Onion, red, chopped
1 cup (250 mL)	Salami, diced
¹/₂ cup (125 mL)	Green pepper, diced
¹/₃-¹/₂ cup (75-125 mL)	Mustard French dressing (page 96)
	Lettuce cups

Quick soak beans (page 13) and cook 1 hour or until tender. Drain. Cook rice in salted water for 25 minutes or until tender. Drain.

Combine beans, pepper, rice, onion, salami and green pepper, stir well. Pour dressing over salad. Stir. Refrigerate at least 2 hours before serving. Spoon into lettuce cups.

Yield: 6 servings.

MUSTARD FRENCH DRESSING

This zippy dressing is good with lentil salads as well as bean salads.

Ingredients

¾ cup (175 mL)	Vegetable oil
¼ cup (50 mL)	Vinegar, wine
1 Tbsp. (15 mL)	Mustard Dijon-style
½ tsp. 92 mL)	Salt
¼ tsp. (1 mL)	Pepper

Combine all ingredients in a pint jar with a tight-fitting lid. Shake vigorously about 1 minute. The oil, vinegar and mustard may be "whisked" together if preferred. Can be stored in refrigerator for 3-4 weeks.

Yield: approximately 1 cup (250 mL)

LENTIL·SPROUTS

A garden-in-a-jar can give you, in 4 or 5 days, crisp lentil sprouts for your hamburgers or a salad of most any kind.

All you need: 1 quart (1.25 L) jar, a square of cheesecloth or a nylon stocking, a rubber band, and 1 pound (500 g) of lentils. You will use ¼ cup (50 mL) lentils for each jar.

1. Wash in a colander or strainer ¼ cup (50 mL) lentils for each quart (1.25 L) jar. Put in a washed jar. Add 2 cups (500 mL) luke-warm water. Fasten the cheesecloth over the top with the rubber band. Let stand overnight.
2. Drain off water.
3. Hold jar on its side. Shake it so that the lentils are scattered along one side of the jar. Lay the jar (on its side) in a dark place like a cupboard or closet.
4. Each morning run luke-warm water into jar. Leave the cloth cover on it. Drain the water. Shake so that the sprouting lentils lie along one side.
5. In about 4 days the sprouts will be about 1 or 1¼ inches (25-30 mm) long and will nearly fill the jar. If you want the sprouts to have little green leaves, put the jar in a sunny window.
6. Take off the cheesecloth and cap the jar. Keep in the refrigerator. The sprouts are best eaten within a week.

SPROUTY EGG AND SESAME SEED FILLING

This crunchy filling is especially good on whole wheat buns.

Ingredients

8	Eggs, hard cooked
¼ cup (50 mL)	Sesame seeds
1 cup (250 mL)	Celery, finely chopped
¼ cup (50 mL)	Onion, minced
¼ tsp. (1 mL)	Pepper
	Garlic salt (to taste)
1 cup (250 mL)	Lentil sprouts
	Mayonnaise, to moisten

Brown sesame seeds, mix with all other ingredients. Moisten generously with mayonnaise. Serve on buns.

Yield: 8 servings.

BUN AND PITA SPECIAL

This mix, full of health giving fresh produce, is a modern version of the old favorite sandwich spread.

Ingredients

6 slices	Bacon, crisp, crumbled
2	Avocados, peeled
2	Tomatoes, medium, sliced
1 cup (250 mL)	Lentil sprouts
	Salt and pepper (to taste)
1 tsp. (5 mL)	Lemon juice
	Mayonnaise, to moisten

Layer bacon, avocado, sprouts, tomato and lettuce into pita halves or buns. Moisten with mayonnaise with lemon juice added. Serve immediately.

Yield: 4 servings.

LENTIL SPROUT TUNA SPECIAL

Ingredients

6.5 oz (184 g)	Tuna, drained and flaked
¼ cup (50 mL)	Sunflower seeds, shelled
1 Tbsp. (15 mL)	Onion, grated
¼ cup (50 mL)	Apple, chopped
¼ tsp. (1 mL)	Basil
2 Tbsp. (30 mL)	Mayonnaise
2 Tbsp. (30 mL)	Yoghurt, plain
6 Tbsp. (90 mL)	Carrot, shredded
¾ cup (175 mL)	Lentil sprouts

Combine tuna, sunflower seeds, onion, apple, basil, mayonnaise, and yoghurt. Open pita bread or buns and fill each with a quarter of the mixture. Top with carrot shreds and lentil sprouts. Chicken or turkey chunks may be substituted for tuna.

Yield: 4 servings.

BEEF AND VEGETABLES

A Chinese meal in itself. The ingredients used are commonly available in supermarkets, except the lentil sprouts. The lentil sprouts you grow yourself.

Ingredients

½ lb (250 g)	Beef, flank or round steak
1 tsp. (5 mL)	Cornstarch
¼ tsp. (1 mL)	Black pepper, fresh, ground
2 Tbsp. (30 mL)	Light soy sauce
3 drops	Sesame oil
2 Tbsp. (30 mL)	Oil for wok
1 cup (250 mL)	Cabbage coarsely shredded
2 cups (500 mL)	Celery, diagonal slices
1	Green pepper, medium sliced
1 cup (250 mL)	Lentil sprouts
	Water Chestnuts (optional)
½ small can	drained, sliced
2 Tbsp. (30 mL)	Water
1	Garlic clove, skinned, chopped
2 Tbsp. (30 mL)	Oil for Wok

Slice beef thinly across the grain.

Marinate beef with cornstarch, pepper, light soy sauce, sesame oil.

Bring wok to high heat, add 2 Tbsp. (30 mL) oil. When oil is hot put in all the vegetables, add 2 Tbsp. (30 mL) water and cover with a lid. Cook in hot wok for 3-4 minutes until steaming. Remove vegetables to a bowl.

Heat up the wok again add oil, put in garlic and beef. Stir fry until beef is cooked, add vegetables. Stir well, adjust seasonings and serve with rice.

NOTE: Slice beef when partially frozen.

Yield: 4 servings.

CHINESE STIR FRY VEGETABLES

There is no nutrient pour-off when you cook vegetables in this way. Oriental spices give them an appetizing and exciting flavor.

Ingredients

2 slices	Ginger, fresh, crushed
1 clove	Garlic, skinned, fat, chopped
3 Tbsp. (45 mL)	Oil
2 cups (500 mL)	Cauliflower, bite size
1 cup (250 mL)	Carrots, thinly sliced diagonally
2 cups (500 mL)	Celery, bite size, diagonally sliced
1 cup (25 mL)	Lentil sprouts
1 Tbsp. (15 mL)	Soy Sauce, light
2 tsp. (10 mL)	Cooking wine (optional)
3 drops	Sesame oil (optional)
½ cup (125 mL)	Water or broth

Add ginger and garlic to oil in a hot wok or fry pan. Add cauliflower, carrots, celery, lentil sprouts, soy sauce, wine, sesame oil, water or broth (broth is better), and pepper. Stir and cover with a lid. Cook with high heat for 5 minutes or until vegetables are done to your preference. Serve hot.

Yield: 6 servings.

SNOW PEA

DENVER SPROUT

This is a quick main dish and an easy meal to prepare.

Ingredients

¼ cup (50 mL)	Butter or margarine
¼ cup (50 mL)	Onion, finely chopped
¼ cup (50 mL)	Green pepper, finely chopped
8	Eggs, beaten
¼ cup (50 mL)	Milk
¼ tsp. (1 mL)	Salt
	Pepper (to taste)
6 oz. (170 g)	Cheese, cheddar type grated
	Lentil sprouts (to garnish)

In a large, heavy skillet gently sauté onion and green pepper in butter until tender. Add mixture of eggs, milk, salt and pepper. Stir over low heat until eggs are partially set. Add cheese and cook until eggs are of desired consistency.

Spoon into pita halves or sandwiches. Garnish with tomato wedges, lentil sprouts, pickles or parsley.

Yield: 8 servings.

TASTE TEMPTING PITA OR BUN STUFFERS

Ham, cream cheese, green onions and lentil sprouts moistened with mayonnaise.

Curried egg salad and lentil sprouts.

Bacon bits, hard cooked eggs, torn spinach and lentil sprouts moistened with mayonnaise.

Turkey and cucumber slices sprinkled with lentil sprouts and served with creamy cucumber dressing.

BREAD·CAKES·COOKIES

Most people like to finish a meal with a sweet and may feel guilty about eating one! However, when the sweets include fruit, nuts and legumes, it adds up to good nutrition.

Protein and other essential nutrients are just as useful when eaten as desserts as they are when served as a main dish.

DATE-LENTIL BARS

Ingredients

⅓ cup (75 mL)	Margarine or butter
1 cup (250 mL)	Sugar, brown
2	Eggs, beaten
½ cup (125 mL)	Lentil purée
1 cup (250 mL)	Flour, sifted
1 tsp. (5 mL)	Baking powder
½ tsp. (2 mL)	Salt
1 cup (250 mL)	Dates, pitted, chopped
1 cup (250 mL)	Almonds, shaved

Beat margarine and brown sugar together, add eggs and lentil purée. Beat again. Add sifted flour, baking powder and salt. Add dates and almonds. Mix thoroughly.

Spread in a greased 9 x 9 inch (22 cm) pan. Bake in a 375°F (190°C) oven for 20-25 minutes. Cut into squares while warm and roll in icing sugar.

Yield: 2 dozen.

SPICE CAKE WITH UPGRADED PROTEIN

Lentil purée upgrades the protein and offers all the other special nutrients contained in lentils. It is still cake, but a cake with special virtues, moist and tasty.

For a 2-layered cake, you will need:

Ingredients

¾ cup (250 mL)	Lentil or split pea purée
1 package (520 g)	Spice cake mix
2	Eggs
1 cup (250 mL)	Water or milk

Grease two 9-inch (22 cm) layer cake pans and follow the package instructions for mixing. Have purée the consistency of canned pumpkin at room temperature. Mix all ingredients together. Bake at 350°F (180°C) 25-30 minutes, or until a toothpick comes out clean. Put together with a favorite frosting or topping.

Yield: 12 servings.

MAGIC HERMITS WITH LENTILS

Upgrade the protein of these cookies with lentil purée.

Ingredients

¾ cup (175 mL)	Margarine or butter
1½ cups (375 mL)	Brown sugar
1 tsp. (5 mL)	Vanilla
1 Tbsp. (15 mL)	Milk or water
2	Eggs
½ cup (125 mL)	Lentil purée
2 cups (500 mL)	Flour
½ tsp. (2 mL)	Baking soda
½ tsp. (2 mL)	Baking powder
1 tsp. (5 mL)	Cinnamon
½ tsp. (2 mL)	Nutmeg
1 cup (250 mL)	Dates
1 cup (250 mL)	Raisins
1 cup (250 mL)	Almonds, shaved

Cream together butter, sugar, vanilla and milk. Add eggs and lentil purée. Beat well. Sift dry ingredients together and use a portion of flour, nuts and fruit. Add remaining ingredients and mix well. Drop by teaspoon on greased cookie sheets. Bake at 350°F (180°C) for 8-10 minutes or until done. Do not over cook.

Yield: 5 dozen.

LENTIL BANANA LOAF

Ingredients

½ cup (125 mL)	Margarine or butter
1 cup (250 mL)	Sugar, white
2	Eggs
1½	Bananas, medium, mashed
4 Tbsp. (60 mL)	Buttermilk or sour milk
½ cup (125 mL)	Lentil purée (page 129)
1 tsp. (5 mL)	Vanilla
2 cups (500 mL)	Flour
1 tsp. (5 mL)	Baking soda
½ tsp. (2 mL)	Salt
1 cup (250 mL)	Walnuts, chopped

Cream butter and sugar, add eggs, beat well. Add well-mashed bananas and beat. Add sour milk and purée mix. Add vanilla and dry ingredients and mix by hand. Add nuts.

Put into a well greased 9 x 5 x 3 inch (22 x 12 cm) loaf pan. Bake in a 350°F (180°C) oven 50 to 60 minutes or until toothpick inserted in centre comes out clean.

Yield: 1 loaf.

OATMEAL-LENTIL CHIP COOKIES

Ingredients

1 cup (250 mL)	Margarine or butter
1 cup (250 mL)	Sugar, brown
½ cup (125 mL)	Lentil purée (page 128)
1 tsp. (5 mL)	Vanilla
2	Eggs
1½ cups (375 mL)	Flour, all-purpose
1 cup (250 mL)	Rolled oats, quick-cooking
1 tsp. (5 mL)	Baking soda
½ tsp. (2 mL)	Salt
½ tsp. (2 mL)	Cinnamon
2 cups (500 mL)	Chocolate chips, semi-sweet

. . . continued . . .

Cream together margarine, sugar and lentil purée. Stir in vanilla and beaten eggs. Combine dry ingredients and stir in. Mix in chocolate chips. Drop from spoon onto greased cookie sheets. Bake in 375°F (190°C) oven, 12-14 minutes.

Yield: about 4 dozen.

NUT BREAD

Use lentil or split pea purée (page 121). This bread makes excellent toast for a special breakfast or slice it and use it for sandwiches with a cream cheese spread. There is a good "crustiness" to these loaves.

Ingredients

1½ cups (375 mL)	**Lentil or split pea purée**
⅔ cups (150 mL)	**Shortening**
2 cups (500 mL)	**Sugar**
4	**Eggs**
⅔ cups (150 mL)	**Water**
2 tsp. (10 mL)	**Vanilla**
3½ cups (875 mL)	**Flour, sifted**
2 tsp. (10 mL)	**Baking soda**
½ tsp. (2 mL)	**Baking powder**
1 tsp. (5 mL)	**Salt**
1 tsp. (5 mL)	**Cinnamon**
½ tsp. (2 mL)	**Nutmeg**
½ tsp. (2 mL)	**Cloves**
1 cup (250 mL)	**Nuts, chopped**

Cream shortening and sugar. Add eggs, beating well, add purée and water. Stir in sifted dry ingredients and nuts. Bake in 2 well-greased loaf pans, 9 x 5 x 3 inch (22 x 12 cm) at 350°F (180°C) for 1 hour or until toothpick comes out clean when probed.

Be sure that the cooled purée is the consistency of canned pumpkin.

Yield: 2 loaves.

LENTIL SPICE COOKIES

These cookies freeze well.

Ingredients

½ cup (125 mL)	Shortening
1 cup (250 mL)	Sugar
2	Eggs
1 cup (250 mL)	Lentil purée
1 cup (250 mL)	Raisins
1 cup (250 mL)	Nuts, chopped
2 cups (500 mL)	Sifted flour
2 tsp. (10 mL)	Baking powder
1 tsp. (5 mL)	Salt
2 tsp. (10 mL)	Cinnamon
½ tsp. (2 mL)	Nutmeg
¼ tsp. (1 mL)	Ginger, ground

Preheat oven to 350°F (180°C). Cream shortening, add sugar and beat well. Add eggs and lentil purée. (The consistency of canned pumpkin at room temperature.) Mix well, add raisins and nuts, flour and other ingredients.

Drop by heaping teaspoon onto greased cookie sheets. Bake until firm to touch — about 15 minutes. Drizzle with lemon icing.

Yield: 4 dozen.

LEMON ICING

Ingredients

½ cup (125 mL)	Icing sugar
½ Tbsp. (7 mL)	Lemon juice
½ tsp. (2 mL)	Grated lemon rind

Cream — enough to make icing soft to drizzle.

CROWD-SIZED·DISHES

Throughout history, food has been associated with major life experiences, such as marriage, births and family and community gatherings to celebrate important events. All of these occasions necessitate appropriate food selection, preparation and service. The sharing of food and drink is symbolic of sociability, warmth, friendliness and communion.

And so it is today, when the crowd gathers the search is on for suitable recipes and many a pie and casserole are carried from one house to another.

It is hoped that some of the following will be useful when it is your turn to feed the crowd.

BAKED BEANS FROM SCRATCH

Tested by the Food Advisory Division, Marketing and Economics Branch, Agriculture Canada.

Ingredients

8 lbs (3.6 kg)	Dry beans (navy)
7 qts (9 L)	Water, boiling
4 oz (115 g)	Salt
2½ qts (3 L)	Liquid from beans
10 oz (300 g)	Brown sugar
3 Tbsp. (45 mL)	Dry mustard
2 cups (500 mL)	Molasses
4 cups (1 L)	Catsup

Wash beans. Add to boiling water. Boil 2 minutes. Let stand 1 hour. Cook slowly until tender, about 2 hours. Drain, reserving 2½ quarts (3 L) liquid. Add the liquid from the beans and all other ingredients to beans.

Turn into a deep 12 x 18 inch (30 x 45 cm) pan. Bake uncovered at 400°F (200°C) until bubbly (30 minutes). Reduce heat to 325°F (160°C). Cover and bake 4 hours.

Yield: 60 – ¾ cup (175 mL) servings.

BEAN FESTIVAL

This is so easy to prepare for the crowd.

Ingredients

3-100 oz cans (3-2800 mL cans)	Beans in tomato sauce
¾ cup (175 mL)	Dry onion flakes
1 cup (250 mL)	Brown sugar
4 cups (1 L)	Catsup
¼ cup (50 mL)	Soy sauce

Combine all ingredients in a large roaster or casserole. Bake in a 350°F (180°C) oven for 2 hours or until bubbling

Yield: 50 servings.

CHILI LENTILS

Ingredients

7 lbs (3 kg)	Minced beef
3-28 oz cans (3-796 mL cans)	Kidney beans
10 cups (2.5 L)	Lentils, cooked
10 cups (2.5 L)	Tomatoes, canned
1 cup (250 mL)	Tomato paste or catsup
3	Bay leaves
6 cups (1.5 L)	Onions, chopped
¼ cup (50 mL)	Sugar
2 Tbsp. (30 mL)	Salt
½ tsp. (2 mL)	Cayenne pepper
¼-½ cup (50-125 mL)	Chili powder, to taste

Sauté the onions and beef. Add the other ingredients, stir, simmer for about 15 minutes, taste, adjust seasoning. Add chili, according to taste and the strength of the chili. Cover and cook slowly for about an hour, on top of the stove or in the oven.

Yield: 50 servings.

LENTILS AND CHICKEN

Ingredients

18–20 lbs (9 kg)	Chicken thighs, breasts
23 cups (5.75 L)	Boiling water
5 lbs (11½ cups) (2 kg)	Lentils
5 cups (1.25 L)	Milk
3–20 tins (3–568 mL)	Cream of chicken soup
4 pouches (6 oz) (170 g)	Onion soup mix

While preparing chicken add lentils to boiling water and simmer gently for 25 minutes. Remove from heat and drain. Brown chicken in skillet or oven until golden brown.

Turn lentils into shallow baking pans. Bury chicken pieces in lentils to half the depth of the chicken.

Add cream soup to chicken drippings; add milk and heat. Pour over chicken and lentils and sprinkle onion soup mix over all. Cover tightly and bake at 350°F (180°C) for 1½ hours or until chicken is tender.

Yield: 50 servings.

LENTIL AND HAM SOUP

Ingredients

3 lbs (1.5 kg)	Pork shoulder, cured, baked
3 lbs. (1.5 kg)	Lentils
1½ lb (.75 kg)	Potatoes, diced
1½ lbs (.75 kg)	Carrots, sliced
2 cups (500 mL)	Celery, chopped
2 cups (500 mL)	Onion, chopped
48 oz (1.5 L)	Tomatoes, canned, chopped, undrained
3	Garlic, fat cloves
4	Bay leaves
1 tsp. (5 mL)	Oregano
2 tsp. (10 mL)	Basil
	Salt (to taste)
3 gals (12 L)	Soup stock
	Mozzarella cheese to top soup

Bake pork shoulder. Remove meat and cube to add to soup later. Use ham bone, juice and stock to make 3 gallons (12 L). Add all ingredients except meat. Simmer 40-50 minutes. Add cubed meat. Skim fat, adjust seasoning. Serve topped with mozzarella cheese. Thin with vegetable stock or water.

Yield: 50 servings.

LENTIL WIENER SOUP

Ingredients

2 lbs (1 kg)	Green lentils, washed
3 gals (12 L)	Soup stock
6 medium	Potato, diced
6 medium	Carrot, thinly sliced
1 lb (500 g)	Onion, sliced, sautéed
10	Wieners, thinly sliced
5	Bay leaves
	Salt pepper (to taste)

Simmer all ingredients in a large soup kettle until lentils and vegetables are tender. Taste, adjust seasonings and consistency.

Yield: 50 servings.

BEAN AND TOMATO CHOWDER

A great New England classic.

Ingredients

2-100 oz cans (5.7 L) (2-2840 mL cans)	Tomatoes
2-100 oz cans (5.7 L) (2-2840 mL cans)	Beans with pork in tomato sauce
4 tsp. (20 mL)	Salt
1 tsp. (5 mL)	Pepper

Combine and heat.

Yield: 50 – 1 cup (250 mL) servings.

CURRIED CREAM OF PEA SOUP

This is a delicately flavored soup using skim milk powder. Very simple to make.

Ingredients

2-100 oz cans (2-2840 mL cans)	Canned peas
	Skim milk powder
5 qts (6 L)	reconstituted
2 cups (500 mL)	Onion, chopped, sautéed
½ cup (125 mL)	Margarine or butter
½ cup (125 mL)	Flour
	Salt and pepper (to taste)
3-6 tsp. (15-30 mL)	Curry powder

Purée the peas in their liquid. Reconstitute the skim milk to liquid. Sauté the onions for 2 minutes. Blend the flour and butter, add a little cold milk to smooth. Add the curry powder, salt and pepper. Combine all together and simmer for 5 minutes.

Yield: 50 servings.

SPLIT PEAS AND CHICKEN

Ingredients

50 pieces	Chicken breasts
5 lbs (2 kg)	Split peas, dry
1½ gal (7 L)	Water, boiling
4 tsp. (20 mL)	Garlic salt
4 cups (1 L)	Onion, chopped
¾ cup (175 mL)	Butter or margarine
¾ cup (175 mL)	Salad oil for browning chicken
4 tsp. (20 mL)	Thyme crushed
2 tsp. (10 mL)	Rosemary
3-20 oz cans (3-568 mL)	Cream of chicken soup or cream of mushroom
1 qt (1.25 L)	Milk

Add split peas to boiling water; boil gently for 2 minutes remove from heat, add garlic salt. Cover and let stand for 30 minutes while preparing chicken.

Cook onion in butter until clear, lift from skillet and set aside. Brown chicken pieces in salad oil and turn into shallow baking dishes. Sprinkle with herbs and spices and spread onion over top.

Drain peas and bury chicken pieces in peas. Add soup to chicken drippings; add milk and heat. Pour over chicken and peas, cover and bake at 350°F (180°C) for 1½ hours. Remove cover for last 10 minutes to brown.

Yield: 50 servings.

CREAMY SPLIT PEA SOUP
WITH MUSHROOMS

This is a delicious variation of a popular soup.

Ingredients

3 lbs (1.5 kg)	Yellow split peas
3 gals (12 L)	Chicken base soup stock
1 lb (500 g)	Onions, chopped, sautéed
2 qts (2.5 L)	Cream sauce, medium
1 qt (1.2 L)	Mushrooms, sliced
	Salt and pepper (to taste)

Add split peas and onions to chicken stock. Cook until peas are soft. Stir cream sauce into soup until smoothly blended. Add mushrooms, adjust seasonings and consistency.

Yield: 50 servings.

PATÉ & PURÉES

This is a small but important section because purées are used extensively in soups and desserts. Be sure that the consistency of lentil and pea purée is similar to that of canned pumpkin, when used in bread, cakes and cookies. Lentil or pea purée may be substituted for pumpkin in recipes calling for canned pumpkin if the flavor combinations are appropriate.

LENTIL PÂTÉ

This is good on toast, flat bread or in sandwiches. The flavor blends well with tomatoes in a sandwich and keeps the bread from becoming soggy.

Ingredients

1	Onion, medium, finely chopped
1 Tbsp. (15 mL)	Oil
1 cup (250 mL)	Lentils
1	Garlic clove, crushed
¼ tsp. (1 mL)	Thyme, dried
¼ tsp. (1 mL)	Marjoram, dried
1 tsp. (5 mL)	Soy sauce, optional
	Salt and pepper (to taste)

Sauté the onion in oil. Add lentils, garlic and herbs. Cover with water and cook 40 minutes or until soft. Drain, add soy sauce and seasoning. Purée.

Yield: 1 cup.

LENTIL OR SPLIT PEA PURÉE

Purée freezes well. Double this recipe and have some on hand to make baked loaves and cookies or use in chowders and soups.

Ingredients

1 cup (250 mL)	Lentils or split peas
2½ cups (625 mL)	Water

Wash lentils or split peas. Cover with water. Bring to a boil and reduce heat. Cover and simmer until lentils are very tender, 30-45 minutes. Drain lentils. Save enough stock to blend with lentils or peas to the consistency of canned pumpkin when cool. As purée forms stop, scrape and mix with a spatula and start blender again until a smooth purée is developed.

Yield: 2 cups purée.

LENTIL PURÉE ON BACON

Ingredients

1 cup (250 mL)	Lentils, washed
2½ cups (625 mL)	Water
1	Onion, chopped, medium
¼ cup (50 mL)	Butter or margarine
	Salt and pepper (to taste)
8 slices	Bacon, cooked

Cover lentils and onions with water in sauce pan and simmer 30-45 minutes. Drain. Blend with a small amount of stock to the consistency of canned pumpkin. Add butter, salt and pepper. Serve spread on cooked bacon slices.

Yield: 8 slices.

GLOSSARY

LENTILS

There are two types of lentils, the large Chilean type and the small Persian type. Lentils are well known as a soup item, but many North Americans are unaware of their more imaginative uses.

Middle Easterners and East Indians know a great deal about how to use lentils to full advantage. Lentils come in different sizes and colors. They range in size from approximately 35-65 grams per 1,000 seeds and in color from red and peach to green and brown.

GREEN LENTILS

Eston, a small Persian type lentil, regular shape with a light green seed coat and a yellow cotyledon. A very good choice for cooking and sprouting.

Laird, a large Chilean type, regular shape, with light green seed coat and yellow cotyledon. If sprouted, the sprouts are larger with a less delicate flavor than Eston sprouts.

Commerical, a medium Chilean type, regular shape, with light green seed coat and yellow cotyledon.

The green lentils may all be used interchangeably in recipes, but the smaller seeded lentils have a more delicate flavor. They are all excellent cookers.

TURKISH LENTILS

A small red lentil commonly available on supermarket shelves. Overcooking makes them mushy; about 10 minutes simmering is enough.

FRENCH LENTILS

A small, slate-green lentil; a good cooker with a pleasing flavor. These simmer to tenderness in 10-15 minutes.

EGYPTIAN LENTILS

Small and salmon pink in color. Like the Turkish lentil, they are commonly available in supermarkets and cook in about 10 minutes.

DRY PEAS — GREEN OR YELLOW WHOLE

Different varieties differ so much in size that it may take from 145-236 seeds to make 1000 grams weight. Yellow peas have a more distinct flavor than the green peas but they may be used interchangeably in recipes.

DRY SPLIT PEAS — YELLOW OR GREEN

Yellow and green split peas are widely available on supermarket shelves. They are used chiefly to make those wonderful split pea soups seasoned with ham, bacon and smoked sausage. They are whole peas that have had their skins removed and then broken in half, so they are more tender than whole peas.

DRY BEANS

Black, a medium sized, regular shape bean with a black seed coat and white cotyledon. Popular for black bean soup and as Feijoada, the national dish of Brazil. A dish called Moors and Christians "Moros y Cristianos" is a West Indian favorite.

GREAT NORTHERN BEANS

Large, regular shape bean with a white seed coat and a white cotyledon. It is the North American version of the Haricot bean and Italian cannellini. When recipes call for Haricot or cannellini, Great Northern beans are appropriate to use.

NAVY (PEA BEANS)

A small, white oval bean, commonly used to make commercial pork and beans. Very popular for home-baked beans and salads.

RED MEXICAN BEANS

Medium, regular shape, with a red seed coat and white cotyledon.

PINK BEANS

Small, regular shape bean with a pink seed coat and white cotyledon.

PINTO BEANS

A large, regular shape bean with a mottled white and brown seed coat and white cotyledon.

RECIPE INDEX

SIDE DISHES

SOUPS

SPROUT DISHES

WEIGHT WATCHERS

LEGUME FACTS AND TIPS

Dry beans have on average 20-25 percent protein, a few varieties with more than 30 percent.

Dry peas are nutritionally considered to be alternates to the meat group. Because they have excellent vegetable protein, only a little animal protein such as meat, fish, eggs, cheese or milk added to the meal plan for the day supplies the missing amino acid to provide complete protein.

Because of their bland flavor legumes combine well with other foods, spices, herbs and blends.

Their special features make legumes useful in high iron, high fibre, diabetic, low sodium and weight control diets.

Most people like to finish a meal with a dessert and may feel guilty about eating one! However, when the sweets include fruit, nuts and legumes, it adds up to good nutrition.

One cupful of cooked dried peas, lentils or beans is equivalent to one serving of animal protein such as 2-3 ounces of cooked lean meat, poultry, liver or fish or two eggs. Being much less costly than meat and dairy food they are economical protein alternatives.